THE WORLD OF
TOYS

THE WORLD OF
TOYS

Dr Josef Kandert

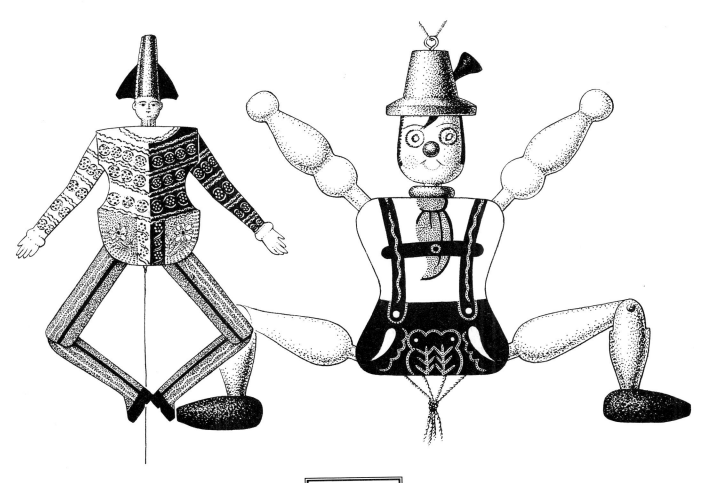

HAMLYN

ACKNOWLEDGEMENTS

The author would like to thank his colleagues of the Ethnographic Museum, the Museum of Decorative Arts and the Náprstek Museum in Prague for their kind help during his research of objects and literature and in compiling the pictorial material, as well as for their revision of the text. The author's gratitude goes also to the CIES in Washington (Fulbright Foundation) for enabling him to visit some private and public collections of toys in the United States.

Text by Josef Kandert
Translated by Joy Kohoutová
Photographs by Jan Pícha
Line drawings by Hana
Sokoltová-Zpěváková
Graphic design by František Prokeš

Designed and produced by Aventinum
English language edition first published 1992
Hamlyn is an imprint of
Octopus Illustrated
Publishing,
Michelin House,
81 Fulham Road,
London SW3 6RB,
part of Reed International Books

A catalogue record for this book is available from the British Library
ISBN 0-600-57478-4
Printed in Czechoslovakia by Polygrafia, Prague
2/09/11/51-01

Contents

Introduction

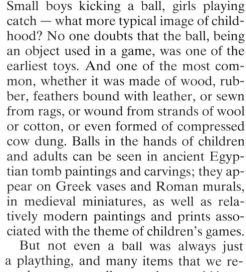

Small boys kicking a ball, girls playing catch — what more typical image of childhood? No one doubts that the ball, being an object used in a game, was one of the earliest toys. And one of the most common, whether it was made of wood, rubber, feathers bound with leather, or sewn from rags, or wound from strands of wool or cotton, or even formed of compressed cow dung. Balls in the hands of children and adults can be seen in ancient Egyptian tomb paintings and carvings; they appear on Greek vases and Roman murals, in medieval miniatures, as well as relatively modern paintings and prints associated with the theme of children's games.

But not even a ball was always just a plaything, and many items that we regard as toys actually served, or could have served, other purposes, as we see from the practices of many different peoples. In the 19th century, the Chukchi of Siberia organized sporting events every year in which the young people competed in running, throwing javelins, and other predominantly male contests. Strangely enough, the victor's prize used to be a decorative leather ball. The winner received it from the hand of the prettiest girl of the tribe who hoped to marry that year.

The character of such a trophy seems less strange when we remember the fairy-tale about the princess bowling an apple or a ball with her swain, or that of the prince who chose a partner by the same 'random' method, a theme which occurs in stories from Indonesia, India, Persia, and Europe. Moreover, this Chukchi gift-ball was stuffed with the hide of the sacred reindeer and both in its form and its decoration it symbolized the giver and reviver of all life on Earth, the Sun. A ball as a Sun or Moon symbol is known from most parts of the world and from many different periods. Ball games welcomed the arrival of the new year among North American Eskimo peoples and the Siberian Koryaks. Members of certain tribes of the Amazon rain forest in Brazil imagined the Sun and the Moon as feathered balls. Similar ideas come from ancient Egypt and many European, Asian and African nations. Sacred balls and ball-toys frequently crop up in ancient myths, usually with religious connotations and often with specific symbolic reference.

A journey into the study of children's toys discloses that across a wide range of time and place many playthings are connected with the intellectual concerns and religious traditions of human beings.

The subject of this book is exclusively 'folk' or ethnic toys: toys produced by and largely for a particular community. As the

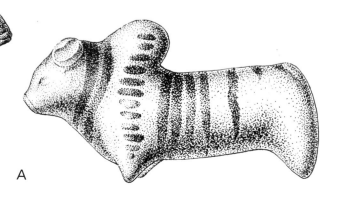

A

1 (A) Fragments of ceramic figures of women and a bull. Culture of the Indus River basin, 2500-1500 B.C.

6

term is used here, folk toys comprise all those children's playthings made chiefly by rural, though also by urban people, which are made by hand and crafted largely, though not exclusively, from natural materials, using hand tools of a simple kind, but not machines.

This book thus differs from most publications about toys, in which folk toys are generally dismissed in an opening chapter or two, the main subject being industrially manufactured toys, especially metal ones. Here, industrial or mass-produced toys are discussed only in connection with the production of folk toys.

The term ethnic relates largely to tribal societies or those of a relatively non-hierarchical structure. Such words as 'tribal' or 'primitive' are often applied to such toys in the literature, although this can be misleading (and not only in regard to production of toys).

Our journey through the world of folk or ethnic toys reveals that the makers of 'primitive' (overseas) and 'advanced' (European) toys followed similar technical principles. As for ethnic toys, the fact that they were hand-made is obvious enough, though the usual corollary, the use of natural materials, is subject to exceptions: instances are known of the use of modern, industrial materials.

One of the problems of defining 'folk toys' is the historical relation of the folk culture of society to so-called 'high culture', or the culture of the elite. In tracing the relation of cultural influences interacting between the elite and the mass of the people, we must always adhere to the following rules.

Study the general historical viewpoint. In various historical periods, depending on the economic, political and ideological concerns of society, the direction of influence — up or down the social scale — changed.

Study the general historical-geographical background. Influences in one or another direction were not the same in all territories of the same continent, sometimes not even in all areas of the same country.

Study the specific producer. It must be taken into account that a number of craftsmen selling their products locally or at neighbouring markets within a certain area worked both for the elite and for the people. In their work they might have followed influences from both cultural milieux. It is especially rewarding to consider this blend of cultural impulses in the products of craftsmen of the colonial period in Latin America, where there was a merging of European, Indian and African traditions. Even in the production of the classical folk toymaking workshops of Central Europe, such as Sonneberg, Seiffen or Oberammergau, the market was spread over several social strata of potential customers. Toys of the same type and model were turned out in different sizes and with different finishing, so that they would be accessible, in price terms, to different social groups.

Study the history of specific products. We come across instances when toys intended for the elite became classifiably folk toys, and the other way around, when folk toys were adopted by the elite. One example of playthings that entered the realm of folk toys from a non-folk origin is the European tin toy. Only in the 19th century, with the growing number of workshops, did they reach the mass of the people in large numbers, although a section of the total production continued to retain the character of toys for the upper class, or even as collectors' objects, intended largely for adults. The most notable example is sets of precisely modelled tin (or 'lead') soldiers wearing the uniforms of individual regiments, with which collectors and war gamers could reconstruct specific historical battles.

Among cases of the elite taking over folk toys, one might mention the little

(B) Three wooden dolls from ancient Egypt. The first is from the Roman period, the other two from the 12th-18th Dynasties. Figures of animals, balls, whip-tops, ships, playing boards and playing stones are also found in ancient Egyptian graves.

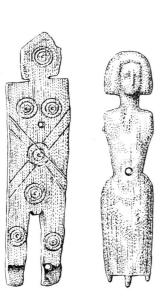

B

2 Doll of calabash, twine and putty, with glass beads. Ngwato tribe, Zimbabwe, before 1880. It represents a type of calabash figure found among many southern African peoples and nationalities. H. 26 cm, d. 7 cm.

wooden horses, originally made in the Swedish historical region of Dalarna, today Kopparbergs Län. Only at the end of the 19th century did they acquire wide popularity, when they were bought, as ornamental objects as well as toys, for households in every town in Sweden, until they finally became a sort of popular symbol of Swedish folk art. Similar instances, in specific types of toys, will be discussed later.

When did the first toys come into existence and what led to their appearance? Did they represent an attempt by adults to make children happy, or did they arise from the playful activities of children themselves? As everyone knows, the spontaneous activities of the young frequently ape the behaviour of their elders, and in each generation the children adopt in their play the objects used by adults for entirely different purposes. The objects stimulate the child's fantasy and inspire games in which they play many quite unexpected roles.

It is somewhat surprising that for an answer to the question of origins we cannot turn to the folklore of the nations of the world, where one finds an explanation for almost everything else provided in fairytales, myths and stories. A tale or myth relating to the origin of toys does not exist and fairytales in which a toy plays the main role are also surprisingly uncommon. Most fairytales and myths about the nature of particular phenomena were intended to bring children closer to the world of adults, to explain things to them, and to advise them of what they could expect in certain social situations. In fairytales, toys appear more frequently in episodic roles — examples being dolls that speak for their owners, give them advice, work and even fight with them, or alternatively cast a spell, and protect with supernatural powers, even kill enemies. In Russia there are fairytales about wooden eagles and ducks that fly, and about other mechanical toys.

Regarding the development of toys in ancient times, our knowledge is restricted to archaeological evidence and occasional documentary evidence. We are aware of different types of toys in ancient history, either through records of their production or images indicating (not always with total clarity) how they were used. But for the most part we do not know who made

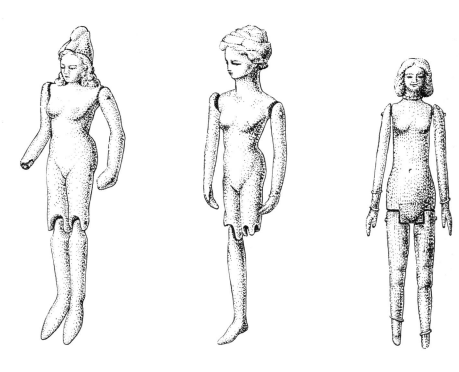

3   Jointed dolls. The first two, ceramic, come from Greece; the third, of carved wood, is from the territory of the Roman Republic, 3rd-2nd century B.C. They have movable arms and legs hung on the same type pins used in folk dolls some 2000 years later.

them or who played with them. The criterion provided by toymaking material is not always a reliable guide either. In a certain country at a certain time, what today is a rare and expensive material, for instance ivory, might have been quite commonplace. We come up against this problem not only with prehistoric toys but also toys dating from the first millennium A.D. Roughly speaking, our knowledge is at best incomplete until the late medieval/Renaissance period. It is only from that

time that we can draw a straight line leading to the folk or ethnic toys of the 19th and 20th centuries.

A survey of the oldest surviving toys discloses both the history of folk toys and the remarkable similarity of toys throughout the world, regardless of who made them or used them.

The occasion of the emergence of toys, as far as we know, must be located in the Neolithic age. But some researchers link the earliest toymaking products to finds of bone whistles, fragments of small figurines and other miniature items from the Mesolithic age. If these claims are accepted we can shift the beginnings of toymaking and toys several thousand years further back into the past.

Archaeologists almost unanimously consider finds of various figurines, models of ships and other items from Mesopotamia that date from about 2000 B.C. as toys, although they do not rule out a possible cult function. Ceramic dolls appear among finds from Harappa (Punjab) of about the same date. Besides the ceramic harnessed buffaloes pulling two-wheeled carts, other objects that are certainly reminiscent of toys come from this early civilization on the banks of the Indus River.

A number of toys — ceramic, limestone, fabric and even wooden — have survived from ancient Egypt. They include wooden dolls and horses, wooden dolls with string hair, and dolls made of balls of twine. Some wooden toys were

4   Noah's Ark, polychrome wood. Exported from Europe to Massachusetts, U.S.A., c. 1800. It resembles a raft with a house. The ark had removable roofs and pairs of animals were placed inside.

movable: the Thebes crocodile and leopard (*c.* 1000 B.C.) had clapper mouths that moved when drawn by a string. Jointed dolls, activated by a cord, ground corn in a hand mill as they moved. These Egyptian toys were found in tombs; the oldest is from the Middle Kingdom, about the period of the 12th Dynasty (from 1991 to 1786 B.C).

Even earlier evidence of toys comes from China, about 5000—4000 B.C. Scholars believe that small bronze objects found in the graves of that period were used as toys.

Larger sets of toys from the first millennium B.C. are known from the first written accounts sof toys. In the Mediterranean area, sets of children's dishes and miniature furniture have survived. We are also familiar with the image of wooden two-wheeled carts, seen on Greek vases, the oldest dating from the 7th century B.C. Ceramic figures of birds, horses,

deer, cows and bulls, goats, sheep, pigs and little dogs, the animals which appear most frequently, are also considered toys. Hoops and whipping tops, which older children played with, have also survived.

Thanks to Greek historians and geographers, we know something about the toys of Classical times. Aristotle mentions figures on wheels, some of which had a religious function. Philostratos analyzed older reports and spoke about Indian figures on wheels. Plato wrote about movable figures. The most important source of information, however, comes from Hero of Alexandria, who lived in the 1st century A.D. and described a number of automata, some of which have been reconstructed in modern times from his descriptions.

Little is known about toymaking centres of those days. It would seem, however, that one was in the town of Sardis, the capital of Lydia, where dolls and ani-

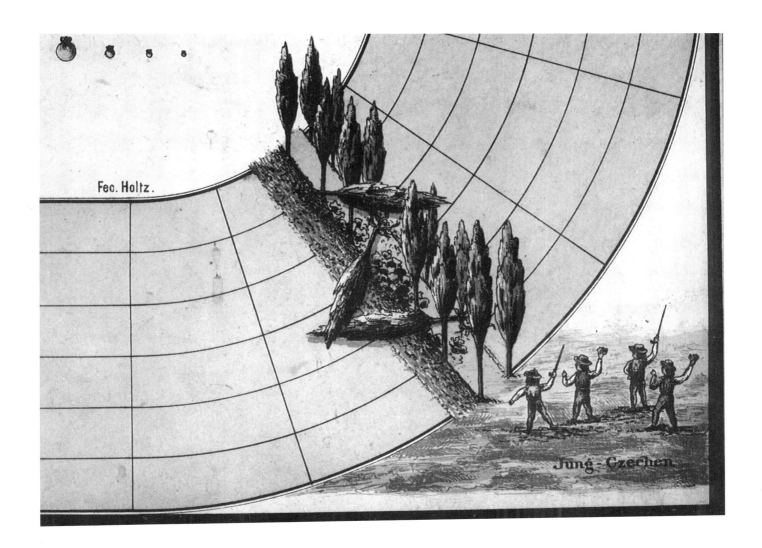

Fec. Holtz.

Jung-Czechen

5 Details of playing boards with race course and four tin figures of races horse. Bohemia, end of 19th century. Playing course is 77 × 56 cm, h. riders 5.7—6 cm.

mals were crafted from wax, clay, plaster and alabaster. Some of these animal figures were also bought by Greek customers for cult purposes.

Toys have also been preserved from the period of the Roman Empire. These include ivory dolls, some with movable arms and legs, miniature lead furniture, little dishes, etc. There are reports of Trojan-horse figures in which little wooden or ceramic Greek soldiers were hidden, which were made and sold in and around historic Troy on what is today Turkey's western seacoast.

From the 2nd half of the 4th century B.C., at a time when ancient Mediterranean civilization was in full bloom, in the Far East the ancient Chinese were already quite familiar with puppets and other toys. On the American continent, too, there existed at that time a civilization, occupying roughly the territory of present-day Mexico, which preserved a number of

toys in graves. From sub-Saharan Africa, knowledge of ancient toys is still scarce, as a result of the small number of archaeological digs and the unsuitable climatic conditions.

In modern times the existence of toys is linked firstly to entertainment and the child's education. It was primarily the educational element of toys that led to the studies of many European teachers, philosophers, psychologists and sociologists, which go back to the 17th and 18th centuries. Among the first to devote attention to toys and playthings were Jan Amos Komenský (Comenius) in the 17th century and Jean-Jacques Rousseau in the 18th. The educational efforts of these two great men were the culmination of earlier development, however. From the 16th century there were general schools in larger towns in addition to exclusively Church schools. The teachers in these schools had to cope with problems similar to the problems facing educators today. The educational importance of toys was a centre of interest in earlier centuries as well.

Among the numerous theoreticians and practitioners who not only systematically classified but also invented toys and games, mention should be made of the German teacher Friedrich Fröbel (1782 to 1852). Together with others, such as Joseph Trentsensky of Vienna, he was responsible for the spread of social games, puzzles and the ever-popular building bricks, among others.

In the second half of the 19th century, publications about toys for the young began to appear in different parts of Europe, aimed chiefly at teachers. Simultaneously, many illustrated books were printed, acquainting children with unknown games, often in the form of nursery rhymes. The steady flow became a flood about the beginning of the 20th century.

While toys contributed to the development of European education, 19th-century literature for teachers and children contained accounts of many folk toys that would otherwise probably have passed into oblivion.

Although the educational aspect of toys is linked chiefly with modern civilization, one comes across educational playthings among tribal societies throughout the world. On the most general level one can say that everywhere young boys imitated their fathers by playing with miniature weapons and tools, while girls played with dolls and imitated the work of their mothers in the family and household.

On one of the islands of what is now Indonesia it was the custom in the 19th century to hold family celebrations as soon as an infant smiled. On this occasion the baby received gifts — different toys for boys and girls. A boy usually received a miniature wooden shield, a wooden sword and a wooden spear — symbols of the future warrior. The girl was given a miniature fireplace made of three stones, a piece of firewood, a palm-leaf fan to start the fire going and bamboo tongs to carry the charcoal — symbols of the housewife.

H. A. Junod has recorded how the girls of Tonga in Mozambique and southern Africa are given their first doll. When the girl asks her mother, cradling a younger sibling: 'Mummy, where did you find her?', she might be told: 'Somewhere in the bush.' And when she asks if she can have a child too, the mother promises to find one for her in the bush. During the next few days, the mother leaves a calabash out to dry, fastens it to a stick, paints on hair and dresses it in rags. The 'baby' doll is ready. If the mother replies to the same question from the little girl, 'I found her in a banana grove,' then the father must cut down a banana stalk and make the leaves into a doll. The material used in creating dolls thus supports the parents' claims about how children come into the world.

A European analogy of this, characteristic chiefly of German-speaking regions, is the wooden figures of little old women sitting on storks, holding babies in swaddling clothes. We know them from more recent products of the Erzgebirge region. They are a response to the traditional explanation of how children come into the world. In northern and central Germany, it is the stork who brings the babies; in Bavaria, Luxembourg and the Tirol the midwife fishes children out of wells or fountains. In other districts, a midwife flying on a stork brings the newborn child.

Besides dolls, balls, hoops, swings, rings and miniature dishes are considered educational toys for girls. All sorts of 'sports' toys or miniature weapons are considered toys for boys: bows and arrows, swords and sabres, spears and pikes, slings, balls, hobby-horses, etc.

The Eskimo of Baffin Land in Canada make harpoons for their sons and the mothers give them pieces of sealskin cut in the shape of a seal, to play with. With their miniature harpoons and spears they can begin to learn to play 'hunting seals', in preparation for adulthood. The same can be said about useful objects that children make for hunting and sports games. For example, the boys of a tribe in Cameroon make fishhooks and plait fishtraps from strips of bamboo to catch fish and crabs.

According to local customs and cultural traditions, educational toys came in a great variety of shapes and forms. In the 19th century it was the custom for Protestants in the United States and Britain to give children special 'Sunday' toys, whose themes drew on stories from the Old Testament, such as Noah's Arks, with their

6   Doll, stained wood.
Ashanti, Ghana, 1960s.
Miniaturized figures of these
dolls, toys and amulets also
appear on some ornamented
combs. H. 34 cm.

sets of wooden animals which at first were imported chiefly from Central Europe but were later produced domestically.

In a certain sense one might consider among educational toys a group mounted on a base of a royal couple and members of the royal court. These appear in Japan on the day of the Girls' Festival. Through play, children acquired a respect for the royal family. A political subtext can be found in other toys. At the end of the 18th century, there were board games promoting the ideas of the French Revolution. A later equivalent is a game of the 19th century: on a course, showing a route leading from Berlin through Bohemia to Vienna, four riders are racing and must overcome a variety of obstacles to reach their goal. One such hindrance is a barricade of hewn trees whereby Czech nationalists threaten the riders.

Wooden or tin figures of soldiers in the colours of famous regiments of European states also had an educational function. We might include among them an American game that marked the centenary of America's independence. It showed a movable figure in 18th-century costume holding the flag of the original thirteen states in its right hand. More recent examples are legion.

A study of the history and development of folk or ethnic toys reveals that educational purposes were not always the most important. An understanding of folk toys helps us not only to learn about the educational views of earlier generations regarding children's playthings, but also brings us closer to their beliefs.

Toys are very often connected with the religious aspect of social life. The wooden statuettes or stylized dolls with round or rectangular heads from the Ashanti of Ghana and other coastal Akan ethnic groups are an example. The dolls, thanks to their alleged supernatural powers, were to protect young girls from evil. Besides this, their appearance was to have inculcated a sense of beauty. During games, however, they were used like ordinary toys. These figures were also symbols of fertility and were worn for luck by pregnant women. The Ashanti dolls thus combined a number of functions.

The brightly painted, richly decorated, stylized wooden figures known as *kachinas* are closely linked to religious rituals of (among others) the Hopi and Zuñi of the south-western United States. They are made by the relatives of children during rituals and one of the masked participants representing the spirit of the *kachina* presents it to the child. The children play with the figures, but a *kachina* placed in the room where the children sleep also guarantees them supernatural protection. Playing with the *kachina* figure has an educational aspect as well. The Hopi and Zuñi know and worship several hundred spirits, all of which assume a different appearance, reflected in the dancers' different masks and headdresses. The wooden figures correspond to the dancers' masks and so, while playing, children learn to recognize the individual spirits.

The Japanese made sets of paper figures, always arranged in two rows. In the back row are ten men and in the front ten women. These sets of figures are linked to the Girls' Festival, whose climax comes on March 3. Each year two such sets usually appear in a family. One, newly bought, is put on a special shelf, while the other, which is a year older, is thrown into the river to carry away all unhappiness with it. The basis for the existence and use of these dolls is a desire by adults to guarantee children a happy life through magic. The dolls sometimes have ceramic heads and in the past they were made not only of paper but also of wood or clay. The best known centre of their production was and is to this day Tottori prefecture, Honshu.

There are European toys, particularly from Central Europe, whose utilization

7 Miniature sickles for casting spells, wood and sheet metal. Included in the set are baskets, hammers, dishes, etc. Bought in La Paz, Bolivia, 1910. L. 8.7 cm and 9.3 cm.

8 'Child's puppet made of a bone and European cloth by Pilagá Indians (Argentina),' says this historical reference of 1904. From Gran Chaco also come miniature wooden dolls which might also have served the ancestral cult. H. 14 cm.

and production are linked to religious holidays, or to a period combining several holidays in one, chiefly Christmas, Easter, All Saints' and All Souls' Days.

Both cult and secular purposes were served, for example, by Nativity figures, but if we do not know the specific circumstances in which they were found, we cannot decide whether they are toys or part of the Nativity scene. Genre figures from some Bohemian Nativity centres such as Příbram and Králíky or German Oberhungen were bought by customers not only in sets but individually, either to supplement a homemade Nativity scene or as children's playthings. In several toymaking centres, toys resembling the Nativity figures were produced for both purposes.

In the Vyatka area of Russia, the dead are remembered on the fourth Sunday after Easter. This holiday is called the day of the 'whistle dance'. While adults danced on graves, sang and often got drunk, children blew the whistles they received as gifts. The name of the holiday indicates that the sound of the whistle probably accompanied the dancing adults. In this instance, it would be difficult to find the primary cult function, which has disappeared almost completely: what remains is only the entertainment of a child's toy. The cult significance of the whistle, although it has long since disappeared, was once more widespread. A whistle was given to children as a gift on important local holidays in various parts of Europe. In Portugal it was given on the eve of the holidays of St Anthony of Lisbon (June 12) and of St Peter (June 28); in Italy (in Vicenza) on the day of SS Peter and Paul (June 29); in Luxembourg at Easter, in Germany and the Czech areas just before Christmas. In Česká Třebová (Bohemia), unglazed whistles in the form of nightingales and cuckoos were sold in the period before Christmas. Believers took them along to midnight mass on December 24, and when the priest proclaimed from the altar, 'Christ, our Lord, is born,' the whole congregation began to blow the whistles. During the remainder of the year the children played with them as toys.

In a number of instances toys did not have a cult function yet were associated with the religious celebrations during which the children received them. Sometimes they were made in the image of a saint and presented on the appropriate saint's day. In Europe and in other Christian countries these are sold on St Nicholas's Day (December 6) and during Advent. Besides toys sold the year round there were also seasonal toys — figures of devils and St Nicholas modelled in plaster, wax, papier mâché or other material. In Bohemia at the end of the 19th century other toys that drew on cult themes, such as figures of nuns, were sold at markets. These were produced in the pilgrimage town of Příbram.

There is a wide range of toys associated with days to honour the dead, such as All Souls' Day in Mexico. Many have an appearance based on the funerary theme of the day. Figures of skeletons, often arranged in groups, of skulls, or of children's graves, are produced.

Toys combining religious and secular functions were common, but some objects became toy or cult items secondarily, after having completed their primary function. The Aymara Indians of Bolivia use during certain ceremonies miniature animals, toy instruments, dishes and clothes made of wood, stone, clay, wool or straw. Participants in these ceremonies believe that those in whose favour spells are cast will obtain all these animals and objects in the course of the year. After the ceremony the objects lose their cult purpose and the children use them as playthings.

At the beginning of this century, the Czech traveller A. V. Frič noticed among the Pilagá Indians of Argentina that some women carried with them bone dolls dressed in clothes. The women even talked to these dolls, but when Frič wanted to buy a doll from them he was unable to. On the other hand, he obtained without difficulty identical dolls that children played with. The reason for the distinction was that the figures kept by the women were souvenirs of a deceased relative, with whom they played as children. After the relative's death, the doll became his or her incarnation and was revered. There are similar instances of a secondary, cult use of toys or of another object in connection with forebears.

Secondary cult functions of a toy can be recognized only by an apparent external similarity or when transferred to another cult environment. In the 19th century the Siberian Mansas, or Voguls, made wooden, bone and metal figures for cult purposes. However, when relations with Russian settlers and traders expanded, people began to buy these cult figures from the settlers. This exchange took place at Irbitsk fairs, where the makers sold the figures as toys. The Mansas, however, used them for their traditional cult purposes.

With the decline in importance of religion among European and non-European nations, one can trace the secularization of a series of cult items — their transformation into objects of entertainment, into ordinary toys.

An example of such a shift in function from the religious to the secular over a longer time span is the use of Easter eggs. Giving eggs in spring is probably part of the ancient religious tradition of celebrating the arrival of spring, rituals ensuring the revival of strength and fertility in Nature and in humanity, which in Christian times became linked with celebrations of Christ's resurrection.

The custom of giving eggs is known throughout Europe and also exists in all countries to which Christianity spread. It has survived to the present day, although its form and inner content have changed. Besides eggs that are painted or decorated in any one of many other ways, gifts today are given which are in the shape of eggs but are actually made of chocolate, papier mâché or perhaps plastic. Nowadays, few contemplate the religious significance of giving the eggs. The act of divine giving has moved to the level of a game for children and young people. The shift to this secular function, however, was documented in the 19th century — a time when the religious importance of Easter and Easter gifts was still universally observed. Ethnographers at the time noted various children's games involving eggs — eggs being used as playthings. Children competed in carrying eggs on a spoon with their arms extended in Germany or Britain, or rolling eggs into a little hole among Lusatian Serbs, the inhabitants of Vamberk and eastern parts of Bohemia; there were contests in knocking eggs against each other in Germany and Moravia, or a competition in throwing small coins against a standing egg in Central and Eastern Europe — from Germany right across Russia.

Other folk objects were secularized in the same way, such as the wooden clappers and rattles which were used on Maundy Thursday, Good Friday and Holy Saturday. In Central Europe the noise made by swinging them around announced noon, the time of benediction, or called people to attend service. Gradually, however, these clappers and rattles, at least the smaller ones, were transformed into toys not necessarily related to Easter.

In other chapters we shall study other specific instances of how the process of secularization of cult items and their transformation into toys developed and shall mention other examples of the close connection between toys and the religions of various ethnic groups.

In studying toys, sooner or later we come to the term 'game' and the problem of the relationship between a toy and a game. We start from the viewpoint that toys and games belong inseparably to one another and that the borderline between them cannot be clearly drawn. Games and toys are intimately related: a game can be played without a toy but an object only becomes a toy through being played with, that is, in a game. If no one plays with it, the best-made toy is not really a toy. Toys of private collectors or museums change from being toys into something else — evidence of the culture of a certain people, tokens of a certain time or place.

The double polarity of 'toy—game' is reflected in certain modern classifications of toys, which are divided according to their roles in the actual game, into toys that are imitative or mediative. During a game with imitative toys, the essence is playing with the toy or making the toy, for instance playing with little dishes. The mediative toys permit the development of some sort of game of movement (for instance, playing with a ball).

During games the child's first knowledge and abilities are evident: playing by itself and with others, using its fantasy, cooperating with other children. In collective play, the personality of a young person is formed. A toy, whether it be a folk toy, a mass-produced one, or an object diverted from some other purpose, is also an important part of the child's external world, a part which prepares and facilitates the child's entry into other external worlds.

In this book, toys are classified according to the material from which they are made. This division by material makes it possible to study in outline the toymaking workshops, most of which were confined to processing a single material, such as wood, metal or ceramics. The disadvantage of such a division is that the same types of toys, made of different raw materials, reappear in different chapters. Dolls, horses, carts, balls etc. were made throughout the world from all sorts of materials. Despite the relatively restricted number of fundamental types of folk toys, and the common principles on which they were made in different places, these playthings represent, on a worldwide scale, such a vast subject that they cannot be encompassed fully in a single book. Therefore the chapters devoted to specific forms of toys, their manner of production and toymaking shops, contain certain omissions. This is the inevitable result of a paucity of evidence, for documentation is absent for vast areas, not merely individual workshops. In the text we have tried to summarize what knowledge there is about these little-known regions of toymaking and to mention the characteristics of the individual areas. More concrete evidence will often be found in the illustrations. The material devoted to the producers of toys was drawn mainly from the Central European region.

The Imagination of Children and the Love of Parents

9 A cow made of
a halved block of wood.
Brdy area, Bohemia, early
20th century. Stylized toys
were made by carpenters
or wood-cutters from
the Tirol, Bavaria, the
Schwyz, Uri and Wallis
cantons of Switzerland, the
Arkhangelsk district of
Russia, as well as the
primeval forests of the
Amazon and the Congo.

Today we can hardly imagine that at the beginning of the 20th century it was a rarity in many parts of Europe to buy a child's toy. Children were left to their own devices or to playthings produced one way or another by relatives and neighbours. This chapter is devoted to those toys — the work of devoted amateurs.

'Take him on without hesitation as an apprentice because he is talented. He was still a small boy when he made little houses from wax, carved boats, fashioned carts from leather and frogs from pomegranate peel.' This, it is said, was the way a citizen of Athens recommended his son as a pupil to Socrates. But regardless of how skilful that son might have been, the father's praise is important as evidence that children themselves played with various materials over two and a half thousand years ago.

Today, the smallest children play with stones, make mud pies, build castles and dig tunnels. They also model or put together all kinds of figures, dishes and im-

plements. The best material for this purpose, throughout the world, is clay or river mud. Let us therefore begin with mud or clay toys.

A great discovery in the last two decades in relation to this subject is the fund of creation by children from various parts of Africa. Figures of bulls and horseback riders from the region of Dakar in Senegal, and the Niger basin in Mali are well known. Riders, tiny people and animals made of clay are also known from northern Liberia, Zambia, Mozambique and the Galla people of Ethiopia. Children of the Zulu and others from South Africa and Mozambique, the Berti of Sudan and the Fulbe of Senegal, built houses and whole villages, as well as figures in clay. Boys from the town of Djénné in Mali create little houses from river mud for their games; from them they put together whole villages or towns. Mud villages and towns are enlivened by bulls, horses, oxdrawn carts, along with cars and motorcycles. Recent archaeological excavation undertaken around Djénné, under the

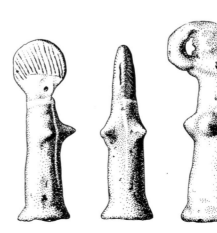

A

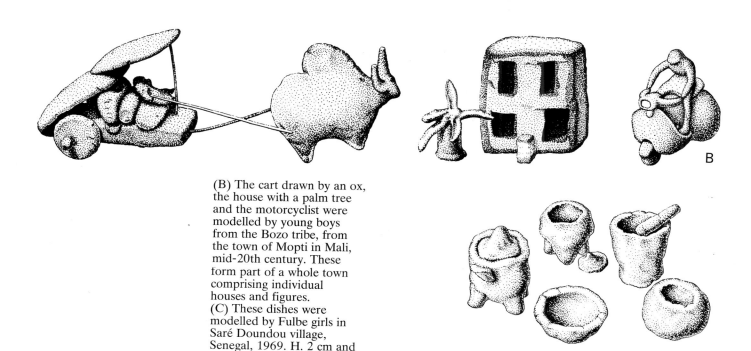

(B) The cart drawn by an ox, the house with a palm tree and the motorcyclist were modelled by young boys from the Bozo tribe, from the town of Mopti in Mali, mid-20th century. These form part of a whole town comprising individual houses and figures.
(C) These dishes were modelled by Fulbe girls in Saré Doundou village, Senegal, 1969. H. 2 cm and 4 cm.

10   West African dried clay toys:
(A) Dolls made by Hausa women and young girls from the town of Anka, Nigeria, mid-20th century. H. 13 cm and 17 cm.

leadership of R. McIntosh, revealed that similar animal figures were made by children more than 17 centuries earlier. Fragments of cows and bulls, sheep and river manatees (sea cows) were found by the archaeologists, stacked in layers, dating roughly from A.D. 300. Of course, the tradition of these figures is even older. There is a set of human figures, pigs, sheep, little dishes, etc. from ancient Egypt, in the Kahun area, which Flinders Petrie interpreted as the work of children during the 12th Dynasty.

In the same areas, and from about the same time, discoveries of earthen dishes were made. Children not only shape all types of vessels they know from their mothers' kitchen, but often build miniature houses to put them into, or entire miniature settlements. There are reports of this from Ethiopia, from the Konso and Galla peoples; from Sudan, the Berti, Dinka and Bari peoples; from Senegal, the Fulbe, and from other peoples of Zambia, Zaire and other parts. Young girls from certain Amerindian tribes in Brazil model earthen dolls, using rubber sap as a binding agent.

Children also use objects found in nature for play. An obvious example is the type of game played under a variety of names throughout the world, and involving stones or pebbles. In Bohemia there are at least 19 versions of this game. Paul Sigrid summarized available reports on it from the African continent and noted a total of seven basic types of game. They included flicking stones from a little pit in the ground, catching them on the back of the hand after throwing them in the air, etc. A survey of ethnic groups indicates how widespread these games are. It is also clear that it is primarily a game for girls, at least in Africa.

The material used changes according to local conditions. In Germany, besides real pebbles, certain bones were used; in 19th-century Armenia these were vertebrae. In ancient Greece and Rome the bones of lambs and cattle were tossed into the air. In southern Africa and Mozambique, the seeds of certain plants were picked out of these little pits; in the Chagaland of Tanzania, when pebbles were not available, children played with fruit or vegetables. Children of the Pilagá of Argentina used pieces of bamboo for the games, while in India they played with seeds as well as pebbles, with polished shards, pieces of enamel, or with beans.

The depiction and reports about tops made of empty snail shells in the area of Nigeria, at the end of the 19th century, indicate how another popular and widespread toy may have come into existence. The shells were weighted at the tip with a piece of lead (such tops were also traditional in China). Today tops and *kachas*

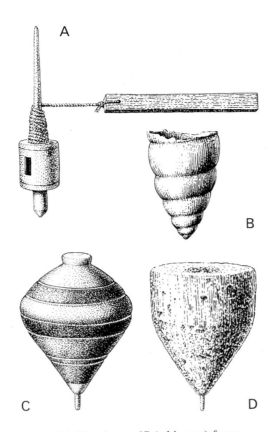

which are close to them, are made in factories on a lathe but in the simpler technology of the past they were homemade toys. The top of course ranks among the oldest toys, and especially among the oldest movable toys. Tops have been discovered in tombs in Thebes from about 1250 B.C.

A kind of top — basically a small Indian club turned upside down and made to spin, is known throughout the world. Its origin is sometimes linked to the spiral forms made by potters. It is spun either by pulling the wound-up thread, or by hand. Among the Tukano tribe of Colombia, boys spin tops by winding strings around them. There are tops of wood and clay, as well as empty shells and, particularly among the forest people of Amazonia, of seeds, fruit and nuts. There is documentation of humming tops in Turkestan and China. In Turkestan their name, 'the sounding marrow', indicates that the vegetable was originally used. At the present time, just as in the recent past, the humming top is only a toy, but in the Mediterranean during the pre-Christian period, it was employed during religious ceremonies because of its humming sound.

The *kacha* does not differ greatly in shape from a top, but it is spun by being whipped. The European *kacha*'s roots go back to ancient Greece and perhaps to ancient India. More likely, however, it originated in the Far East, possibly Japan, where most toys of this type have survived. We know of several dozen such toys from Japan, compared with five to eight from Europe of comparable age. It is also possible that many types in the Far East, in contrast to Europe, came into being only because they proved such favourites.

11 (A) 'Buzzing wolf' (whip top) from Qara Chodzha in eastern Turkestan, China. H. 15 cm.
(B-D) Three spinning tops. The snail shell (B) is from Garua, Nigeria, 1895. H. 3.5 cm. The painted example (C), wood with polychrome decoration, is from Mexico, before 1982. H. 8 cm. The plain version (D), wood, is from the coast, Tanzania, 1960s. H. 7 cm.

12 (A) Ancient Egyptian fabric balls, 2000 BC., the surface was painted or overlaid with painted reeds.
(B) Balls plaited from strips of pandan palms are from the Ellice Islands, western Polynesia, early 20th century.
(C) Turkestan (China) ball of silk and wound cotton thread, early 20th century. D. 8 cm.

A

B

C

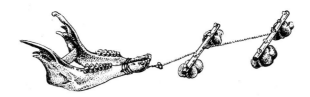

13 Cart drawn by two pairs of oxen. South Africa, mid-20th century, made from a cow's jawbone and knucklebones. Knucklebone oxen are also used by children in Matabeleland, Zimbabwe. From the same area come clay ox wagons and carts made of wooden chips.

Besides the ordinary spinning *kacha*, there were more complicated versions. For instance, at the end of the 19th century Japanese children played a game known as 'a trap for the fox'. The *kacha* was caught in a noose or a snare.

The top, including the *kacha* form, was also known in Oceania where young men as well as boys on the Solomon Islands enjoyed making it spin.

Another very widespread homemade toy is the ball. It is usually plaited from maize leaves by the Indians of Peru and

Ecuador, from palm leaves in the Gilbert Islands in Micronesia, or wound from wool or cotton in Armenia, Turkestan, China, Korea, and Japan. It is also made of rags, cowhide or other animal pelts in Bohemia, Hungary and northern Liberia. There are feather balls for a game similar to badminton in Botswana and Namibia. Children in South America played with round stones as well as wooden balls, particularly the Mapuche of Chile and the inhabitants of Gran Chaco. North American Indian children used leather balls, but the ceramic balls of ancient Egyptian tombs can be considered the oldest of all.

While one type of toy appears in many materials, a whole range of others are made of one material only.

We mentioned earlier the sheep bones used in ancient Greece as playthings. Bones also formed the basic construction material of dolls with which children played in Gran Chaco, Paraguay, Bolivia and Argentina. Animal jawbones and vertebrae belong in this category. The Museum in Linz owns a sledge drawn by two pairs of oxen obtained from South Africa in which the sledge is made of an animal's jawbone while the oxen are formed from vertebrae. Jawbones dressed in rags represented camel riders for the Tuareg children of the Sahara.

Children made little sailing boats from leaves, especially palm leaves, in Tahiti, the Ellice Islands of Polynesia and the Trobriand Islands in Melanesia. Palm leaves were also used to make windmills or a sail that the wind blew along the

14 Toys using the force of the wind:
(A) Kites made of palm leaves, Ellice Islands, western Polynesia, mid-20th century.
(B) Pinwheels of wood with polychrome decoration are from Wadimu region, Papua-New Guinea, early 20th century.
(C) Pinwheels of coconut palm leaves come from the Ellice Islands, western Polynesia, 20th century.
Similar types are found in Europe.

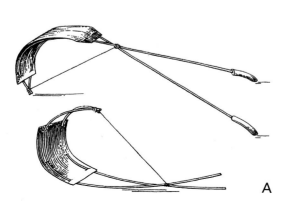

A

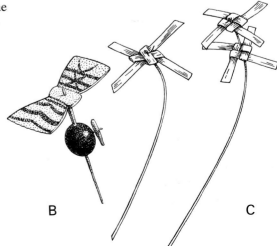

B   C

A

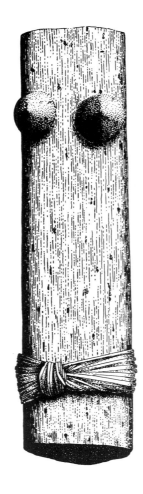

B

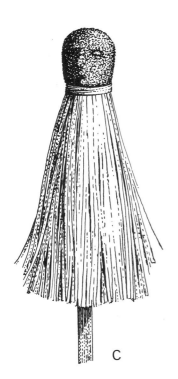

C

15 20th-century Brazilian dolls made of very different materials:
(A) plaited bast; in Siberia figures were plaited in the same way.
(B) palm stalk with modelled wax breasts, Canello, Brazil.
(C, D) with heads of natural asphalt, Karazha, Brazil.

beach. From fallen, brightly coloured leaves, especially from oak trees, Central European children constructed kites, belts, kilts and baskets.

Other popular materials are the fruits and seed pods of plants. In the European temperate zone, animals and figures of people were formed from pine combs, acorns, rose hips and chestnuts. Boys made pipes from acorns and chestnuts, while girls made dolls from empty poppy pods. These same fruits could also serve as playing stones. But the lifespan of fruits and seeds is relatively short; they serve only until they rot or break. Therefore dried fruits were also used. Rose-hip and dried-plum figures appeared in Central European countries at St Nicholas markets — at a time when rose hips were picked and when the first dried plums came out of the drying house. A doll made of dried figs and dressed in fabric clothes has also survived from Calabria in Italy.

Wherever maize was grown, girls made dolls of maize ears, some of which they dressed. Empty maize ears were also used as material in preparing other toys; for example, in the Parapiti River basin of Gran Chaco, young boys added a wooden shaft and feather 'wings' to the end of the empty ear, making spears to throw at a target.

In North America, Indian children used the dry maize husks to make swaddled figures. Children of European colonists recognized this toy, and there is information from the 18th and 19th centuries of dolls made of dried maize husks. Dolls and animals were produced in Central Europe, particularly Moravia, Slovakia, and Hungary, from these leaves and from straw. We have other evidence of this from the then Yugoslavia, Mexico and Brazil. In places in Hungary, toys were fashioned not only from ears and husks of maize but also from the stalk, which, for instance, was made into an ox-drawn cart or a little fiddle (Szolnok area). Among peasant farmers one is not surprised at the use of rye or millet straw; one might mention here millet-straw plaited dolls from Zanzibar. Children also were able to use potatoes for their games. In Bohemia they made hand puppets from potatoes and played with them in toy theatres.

South America is a region notable for the use of organic materials for toymaking. Dozens of dolls and animals made of dried maize husks, straw, palm leaves, little sticks and combinations of these materials are housed today in museums around the world.

From the dried husks of melons, marrows or calabashes came dolls, masks, scarecrows, etc. In colonial New England, scooped-out pumpkins were children's toys; holes were cut for eyes, nose and mouth, and a lighted candle was placed inside. This apparition had a special name 'Jack-o' Lantern', then used as a term for harmless lunatics. Such lanterns are still made at Halloween.

Girls in Mozambique and southern Africa used round calabashes as balls. In

22

China, carved rattles were made of dried marrows, as well as little dishes and figures.

A classic toymaking material is wood, or tree bark, which requires a tool of some sort — at least a knife. Small boats, carts, whistles, and stylized models of rifles and pistols were made of wood. From branches of softwood trees pistols and whistling peashooters were made in lands as far apart as Central Europe and Indonesia. Appropriately bent willow branches substituted for more expensive hobby horses. Such a substitute, made of a curved length of willow rod, is known from western Hungary.

Among movable wooden toys were little mills, placed in a stream or millrace and turned by the current. Toy shovels were fastened to empty spools of thread or to split sticks in Bohemia, Moravia and Slovakia. Today, children in many parts of the world construct motor cars or lorries of boards and sticks. Some African models of this type have already found their way into the angiques market.

The great variety of carts demands a special chapter. Some are so small that they can carry only a tiny load, but quite often children make cars or little carts of such a size that they can ride in themselves. From northern Liberia and northern Nigeria there are various models of one- and two-wheel carts that children either pushed, with a passenger in front, or pulled. A more modern variant is the go-cart built of an old baby carriage. Home-made scooters, sledges or the precursor of today's bobsleigh can be included among vehicles. A wooden seat fastened to a barrel stave was used in colonial North America and known as a 'jump-scooter'. One more modern version in Bohemia is a seat attached to ice-skates.

Children made various wooden 'sound toys'. In England in the 1870s, two sticks of wood, one flat and the other jagged, were used when playing blind man's buff. By passing the smooth wood over the jagged piece, a sound similar to a rattle resulted, thus attracting the blindfolded player. Wooden rattles were a favourite toy of the children of a number of ethnic Indian peoples in both Americas, for instance, among Eskimo of central Canada, the Choco of Panama, and the Chané of Gran Chaco. Rattles in the form of but-

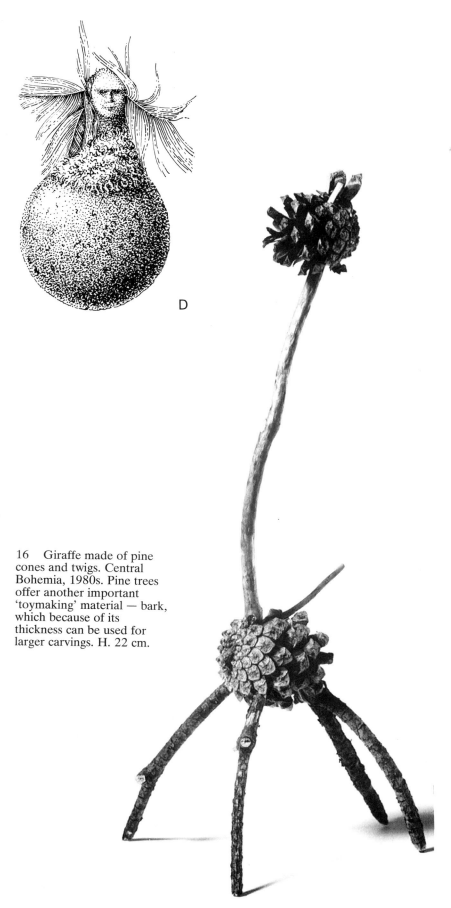

D

16   Giraffe made of pine cones and twigs. Central Bohemia, 1980s. Pine trees offer another important 'toymaking' material — bark, which because of its thickness can be used for larger carvings. H. 22 cm.

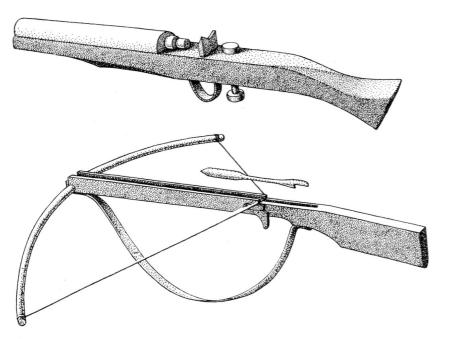

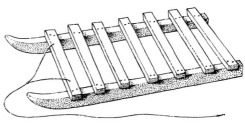

18   Miniature sledge of driftwood found by Eskimo children on Baffin Island, Canada, before 1984. L. 42.7 cm.

17   Pistol and crossbow. Probably Skašov, Bohemia, 20th century. The pistol has a lead spring.

19   Cutting weapons:
(A) Dagger, stained wood. Kuba tribe, Zaire, before 1949. L. 41 cm.
(B) Small sword sold at a fair in Mexico, 1982. Its hilt is of plastic and on the wooden blade is a painting of a miraculous swordsman. L. 45 cm.
(C) Wooden sword with polychrome decoration from China, before 1956. L. 20.6 cm.
(D) Small sword from Nubia, Egypt, 1960s, made of wood, colourful fabric and aluminium foil wound together. L. 36.5 cm.

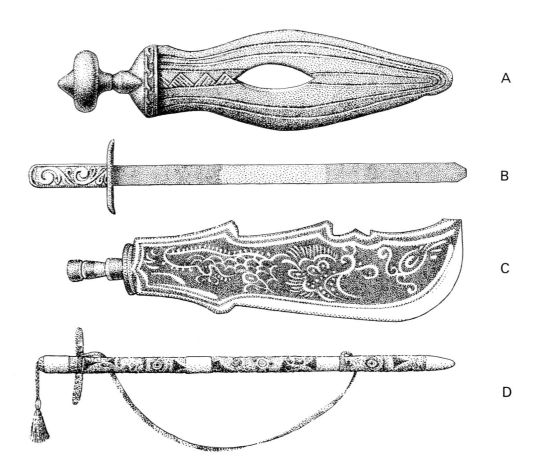

A

B

C

D

20 The world of children's toys includes not only clay animals and houses but model radios as well. This one came from Nag Mansour Kuleig village, Nubia, Egypt, in the 1960s. The children played with the latest model, judging from its design, a transistor radio with clay batteries. H. 20 cm, w. 13.5 cm.

tons strung on a thread are also found in Africa, in Togo, among the Fang of Cameroon and in Central Europe.

Another sound-making toy is a type of 'telephone'. There is a description from Madagascar, in 1880, of one variant of this toy. The telephone was created from two bamboo sticks, each covered at one end with thin skin, and joined to the other by a string. The children spoke to each other through the open end. At the beginning of the 20th century this same toy was found among certain tribes in Cameroon.

Mention has been made several times that children used the artefacts of adult society to make toys. Among these were swords and crossbows made of housing shingles in Bohemia and dolls crafted from old shoes or bedroom slippers in very deprived areas of Britain before the 1914—18 War.

A material used for girls' toys is cloth or fabric. Not only do they make dolls' clothes from it, but often also the dolls themselves. Besides the familiar rag-dolls, they make dolls with stuffed bodies covered in cloth.

Paper is used for a great variety of amateur toys. An obvious example is the kite. According to some accounts the kite was invented around 400 B.C. by a Greek named Archytas of Tarentum, but there are reports of kites flown in China at only a slightly later date, about 220 B.C. It seems that the present popularity of the kite derives more from the Far Eastern tradition than that of the Greeks. In China, a common variant of the paper kite takes the form of a dragon, as perhaps it did in the Middle Ages in Europe (kites are shown in a miniature from a German manuscript of 1405). A woodcut of a kite appears in a book by John Bates, *The Mysteries of Nature and Art* (1635). Similar types appeared later in India where kites were sometimes made to fight a duel in the air. The strings to which they were fastened were dusted with powdered glass and each one tried to cut his opponent down. In Japan in the 19th century, paper kites were decorated with painted portaits of famous samurai or printed historical scenes. A kite made of palm leaves was characteristic of Polynesia.

21 Goat's jawbone forms the basic material of 'camels' which boys in Hilla Duda village, Berti, Sudan, assembled to form a caravan in 1965. Each of the camels is saddled and sometimes carries a load. H. *c.* 20 cm.

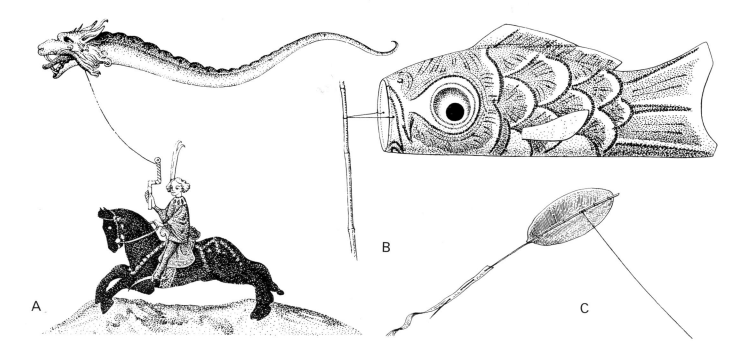

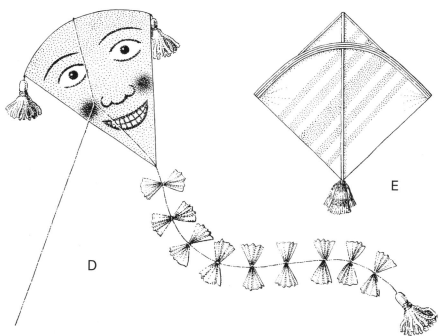

22 (A) The oldest known European depiction of a kite. Germany, 1405.
(B) Similar are Chinese kites or Japanese carp, hung in front of the house on the day of the Boys' Festival.
This carp is from 1925. L. 60 cm.
(C) The palm leaf kite comes from the Ellice Islands, western Polynesia.
(D, E) Kites from Bohemia, 1960s, h. 85 cm, and from India, 1920s, are both of painted paper.
Rectangular kites with two 'heads' were also used — for instance in Lusatia, eastern Germany.

Among other paper toys are pop-ups, usually figures of animals, people or various objects. There are heads of devils and crows, of 'swallows' that move their wings, and darts or arrows. Children associated paper pop-ups worn on the fingers, which opened and closed as the fingers moved, with the idea of fortune telling. According to tradition they would tell whether a playmate would go to heaven or hell after death. Modern variants merely describe the character of the playmate.

Another movable — folded and cut — paper toy is the windmill or pinwheel, usually attached to a stick, which turned in the wind like a full-size windmill. They have been common since the 19th century in Central and Western Europe, and are known by a great number of regional names.

The Japanese, characteristically, made folding paper into an art form. They produced dozens of instruction books on this ingenious craft. At the present time books are still being published on this art, which is known as *origami*.

The paper dolls called *anesama* from Japan are a variation of paper pop-up toys. They were usually made by older girls for their younger siblings.

At the end of 1978 UNESCO mounted an exhibition of children's toys at which many toys made by children were on display. These included carts made of tin cans from Mali, wooden bulls on wheels

23 Folding paper toys:
(A) Small red deer. Japan, 20th century.
(B) Trousers. Bohemia, 19th century.
(C) Crab. Japan, 20th century.
(D) Boat. Bohemia, 19th century.

from Nigeria, animals made of corks and bottle stoppers from Argentina, little huts made of palm leaves from Venezuela, rag animals from Ireland and Jamaica and dolls of all possible materials from many countries. Empty tins and wires were employed in the production of toys in southern Africa among the Zulu, Xhosa and Sotho.

A greater number of toys were produced by adult amateur toymakers. In mountain and forest areas, animal and human figures are commonly produced from roughly cut or carved sticks, split stakes or logs. They are often made to look like cows or horses. These come most notably from Germany, around Kandern, from the cantons of Uri, Schwyz and Valais, in Switzerland, from Bohemia, and the Arkhangelsk region of northern Russia.

Toys related to hunting, military weapons, and sports toys form a large group of the playthings produced by adults. The list might begin with the bow. Among most American Indian tribes, up to the

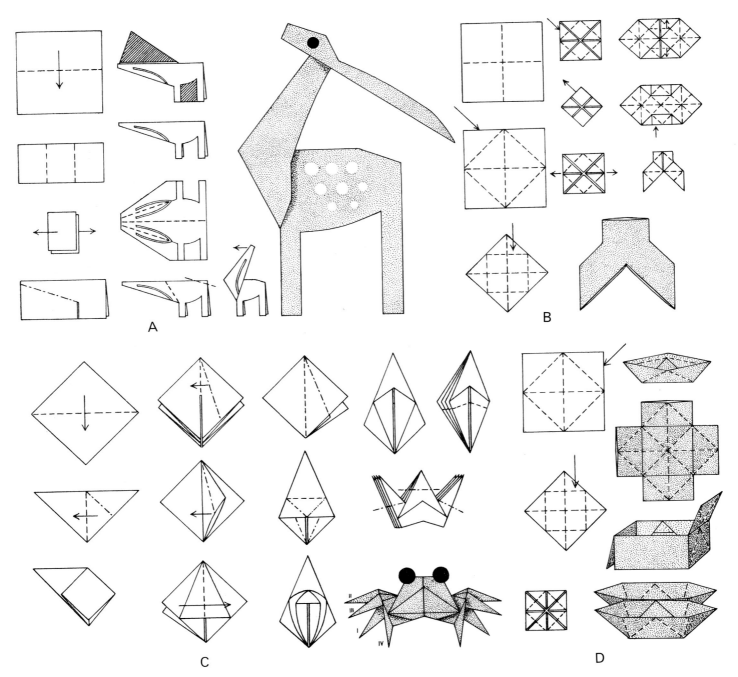

A

B

C

D

24   Painted paper dolls
known as *anesama*
(older sisters) from Japan,
before 1925. Sometimes
their faces lack features,
but their traditional hairstyles
are always meticulously
arranged. There are several
costume variants: dolls from
Yokote are stiffened with
sticks so that they can be
stuck into the snow; dolls
from Tokyo have elaborate
coiffures made of white
crepe paper; dolls from
Kochi have clay faces and
paper hair.
H. 19.5 cm and 23.5 cm.

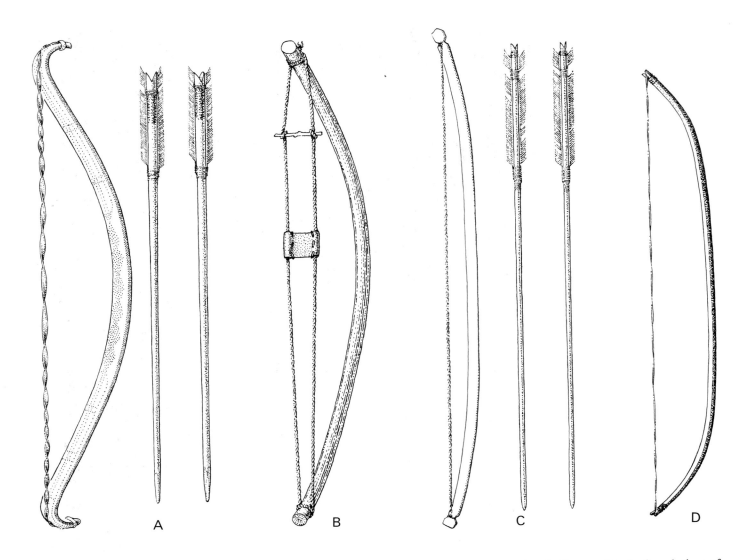

25 Wooden bows and arrows.
(A) Nevada, U.S.A., before 1889. L. 88 cm.
(B) Qara Chodzha, eastern Turkestan,
China, early 20th century. L. 39 cm.
(C) Mexico, before 1982. L. 55.5 cm.
(D) Southwest U.S.A., 1930-31. L. 68 cm.
The Turkestan toy uses the bow principle but
fires clay balls in the same way as
a slingshot. Length of arrows ranges from 50
to 55 cm.

late 19th century, it was still the type of gift that most young boys received. The youngsters not only went hunting for small animals with their bows, but also held their own archery contests. Bows as toys are to be found also in Indonesia, among Asian countries and in Africa. From Turkestan, apart from the usual bows and arrows, we know of bows that shoot clay balls — a kind of variation of the slingshot. In the rain forests of South America the children's blow-pipe is known, in addition to the bow. About the beginning of this century there were reports of Japanese blowpipes and small arrows for shooting at a target. Among children's 'shooting' weapons, mention should also be made of the spring pistols and rifles from which beans and various seeds are shot. Sometimes bamboo strips are used for a spring. These are found in the Parapiti River area of Paraguay, among The Zuñi of the U.S.A. and in some African countries, for instance Togo, Cameroon and Tanzania.

Slingshots are classified among military and hunting weapons. They are known today from the forest regions of Colombia, Venezuela, Ecuador and Peru, from the Peruvian mountain Indians, from the Fulbe people of Senegal and from Spain, among other places. Besides the normal

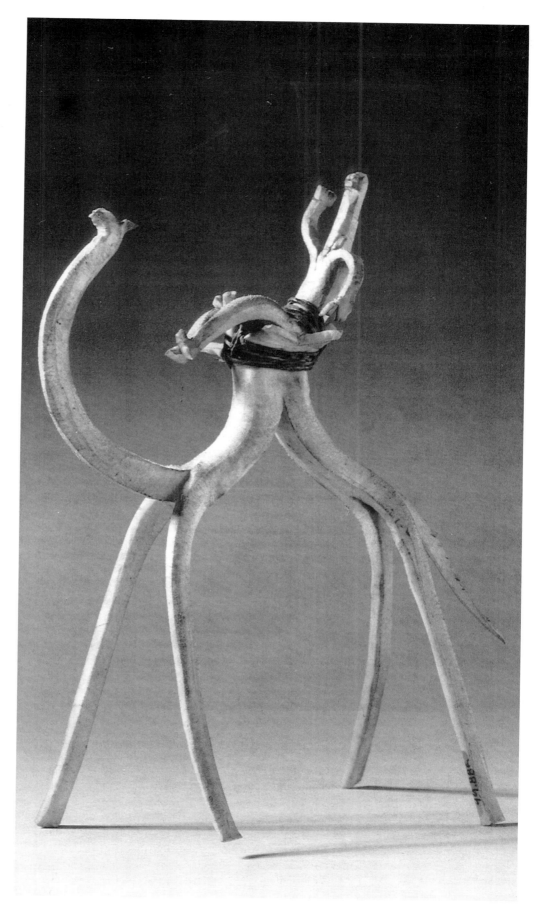

26 Camel and rider, one of
few toys carved from the
hide of wild animals. Niloti,
southern Sudan, before
1939. H. 20 cm,
w. 17 cm.

27 Central African variant of toys modelled very simply from sticks, representing the figure of a hippopotamus (?), acquired from the Pygmy Epulu tribe, Zaire, at the end of the 1940s. L. 44 cm, h. 14 cm.

sling, usually made of leather straps or cords, there is also the forked, elastic sling better known as a catapult.

Somewhat similar toys also occur in a much more limited area. One example is a type of projectile called *bolas* found only among children of the Che peoples in Argentina which in its adult form was once a weapon of war. Another is a boomerang, which may be either curved or cross-shaped. Some boomerangs are of the kind that return to the thrower, unlike the adult hunter's boomerang which does not return (regardless of whether the target has been hit). Curved boomerangs come from all over Australia; the return-type, cross-shaped boomerangs are indigenous only to north-eastern Queensland. They do not differ greatly in shape from the genuine article but are naturally smaller and lack the religious decoration of the adult weapon.

Stilts are popular practically everywhere. They are well known in Mexico and the south-western states of the U.S.A., among the Shoshoni and Hopi Indians, in the Xingu River basin in Amazonia, in Guyana, the Ellice Islands of Polynesia, Japan and China, as well as Europe. In China, children played with stilts in the 12th century. In Europe they appeared around the 13th century. They were also known, of course, in pre-Columbian America.

Children rolled hoops in ancient times as they still do. In ancient Greece adults organized hoop races for children. Hoops appear in an early medieval illuminated manuscript, though in Europe their popularity only reached its height in the 19th century. We also know of them on other continents. There is a picture from 1885 of young Japanese boys rolling hoops. Children of the Pueblo Indians in the south-western United States trundled hoops around in the 1930s, and no doubt earlier.

Some playthings and games were used equally by children and adults. Besides being a form of entertainment, they were also tests of skill. Among these are the cat's cradle, which consists of forming patterns by looping and pulling threads or strings around the fingers and palms of both hands.

Whereas in Europe today these are only children's games, in other continents they are still a form of adult entertainment, and in contrast to the European version, a great variety of patterns is

28 Ceramic doll, painted with distemper.
Mohave tribe, U.S.A., before 1914.
Archaeological finds in Utah document the
existence of almost identical figures more
than 500 years ago.

29   Sealskin ball decorated with leather
appliqué — a contest trophy. Chukchi,
Siberia, before 1911. Its decoration is the
sun motif, found on hliday dress, head
bands and purses/pouches of several
Siberian nations. H. 12 cm, w. 13 cm.

30   Podium with figures of the Japanese
royal couple and members of the royal court,
wooden slats with polychrome decoration,
before 1925. Stylized or rustic forms of
podiums are installed at the Girls' Festival.
L. 17.5 cm, h. 11.8 cm.

31 *Kachina*, wood with
polychrome decoration.
Hopi, U.S.A., 1920s. The
name *kachina* is also used
for the spirits they represent
and for dancers in the masks of
the spirits. H. 21 cm.

32   Devil in the shape of a tinker, plaster and fabric, bought in Prague at a pre-Christmas market in the 1870s. It recalls the pedlar and hawker dolls that were favourites in England in the middle of the 19th century. H. 34.5 cm.

34   Dolls made of maize ears and fabric.
Saré Doundou village, Fulbe, Senegal, 1969.
Made by children. H. 11.5 cm and 18 cm.

33   Knitted woollen purse
decorated with motifs of
llamas and birds. It was
bought in 1910 together with
other miniature animals and
utility items at an Indian
market place in La Paz;
originally it was intended for
practising sorcery.
H. 11.5 cm, w. 7.5 cm.

35   Rag doll, made by
children. Lomé, Togo,
before 1983. The skirt is of
bast, the eyes of cowrie, the
hair of horsehair.
H. 39.5 cm.

36 Slingshots were used by boys not only to play with, but also for hunting and in the fields to drive away the birds when the grain was ripening. They were both a toy and a weapon in ancient times. They are also found in the New World. Children's woollen slingshots were discovered in the graves of the Nazca culture, Peru, A.D. 300-600.
(A) A woollen slingshot from the Mapuche tribe, Coipuco village, Cautín province, Chile, before 1972. L. arm 57 cm.
(B) A sisal slingshot from the Fulbe, Saré Doundou village, Senegal, 1969. L. arm 93 cm.

formed with the strings. The game was played by Eskimos, who made several dozen patterns and held organized contests, as well as by the Indians of Amazonia, the inhabitants of Polynesia and the most varied ethnic groups of Asia and Africa. From India there is evidence of ritual use of these looped patterns, involving two or three strings. The patterns represented religious symbols, just as the patterns formed solely for entertainment are imitations of objects, such as a chair, a cradle, a set of candles, a trident, etc., or of stylized animals such as a crab, a sea serpent, a fly, a monkey's paw, or of natural phenomena like stars, a river, a mountain or the sunset. Although most of these involve looping the strings only around the palms and fingers, in some societies, for example in Wadi Halfa, Sudan, the feet are also employed.

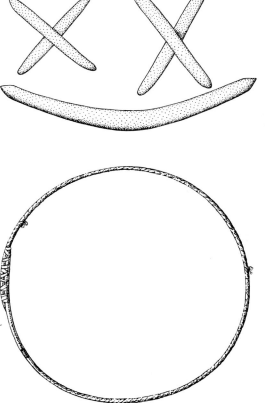

A

B

37 Wooden boomerangs for sport and play from Queensland, Australia, 19th century. The crosses belong to the type that returns, both arms being tied before being thrown; the rounded type does not return.

38 Hoops of twigs and string driven by a stick were used in the 1930s by Indian children in the Southwest U.S.A. D. 50 cm.

39 There are many 'cat's cradle' figures made of thread or string; although similar, their names differ because each ethnic group sees something else in the same patterns.
(A) The fish-trap is from the Patamona tribe, Guyana, early 20th century.
(B) The trouser legs are from Scotland, early 20th century.
(C, D) The young girl and the monkey's tail come from eastern Nigeria, early 20th century.

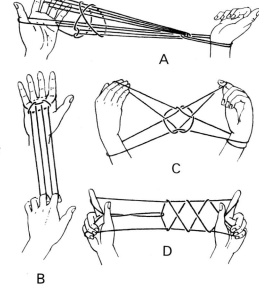

A

C

B

D

41

40 Ship model made of reed and wood by the Aymaras, Suriki Island in Lake Titicaca, Bolivia, before 1964. It is equipped with a double paddle, tripod mast and miniature fishing net, just like a real ship.
L. 83 cm, w. 12.6 cm.

Cut-outs are another example of playthings employed by children and adults. The most popular and probably also the most widespread were those of the Far East, especially China and Vietnam. Here they are not just toys but also a method used by adults to decorate their dwellings. Examples of cut-outs made by children and adults occur in Russia, Poland, Slovakia and Mexico. However, in Europe they appeared only in the 18th century, much later than in the Far East, and if we do not include machine-printed paper dolls and clothes as produced in

41 (A) Wooden catamaran from the Gilbert Islands, Micronesia, end of 19th century.
(B) Wooden catamaran from the Truk Islands, Micronesia, end of 19th century.
(C) A wooden raft from Tetua, Nonouti, Gilbert Islands, Micronesia, end of 19th century.
In the past such ships were used for fishing in lagoons. They have only survived in the form of toys.

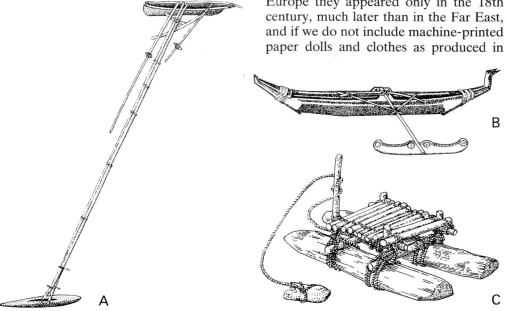

large quantities today, they never really became a folk toy.

A comparison of the toys made by children and those made for children by amateur toymakers reveals that they do not differ so much in type as in the method of manufacture. The Fulbe girls of Senegal, for example, made dolls from maize ears, whereas their parents produced more complicated dolls from beeswax and clay; this composition made it easier to model the doll's head and body. In Mauretania, instead of using wax for modelling, they used a paste made from peanuts. While the children of the Ellice Islands of Polynesia fashioned little boats of palm leaves (also found in the Shouten Islands and Tahiti), their fathers made more accurate models of rafts and ships out of sticks. From Lake Titicaca in Bolivia come models of reed boats made by reed boatbuilders for their children. Today these models are sold as souvenirs. The accuracy with which model toys were made often compares well with the genuine article.

If in certain areas miniature cultural objects were produced for children as toys and for adults as models or ornaments, they usually differed in the degree of stylization. The toys were, naturally, simpler. For example, on Wuvulu Island of Me-

42 Doll with a leather head, fabric body and dress, wearing glass beads. Eastern Dakotas, U.S.A., before 1929. H. 28.5 cm.

43 Leopard and antelope, figures made of dried meat and covered with animal skin. Hausa, Nigeria, 1970s. Children of many Sahel tribes play with these types of figures and museum collections document their existence since the 1870s. H. 10 cm, and 10.8 cm.

44 Stained wooden scooter made without a single nail. The two nails on top are used as hooks but do not keep the construction together. Ibanda village in the Ruwenzori Mountains, Uganda, before 1980. The same type of construction is also found in Kenya. H. 78 cm, l. 94 cm.

45 (A) So-called hen, dried clay and leather strap. Eastern Turkestan, China. H. 9 cm.
(B) Balance, wood with polychrome decoration and metal. Quebec, Canada, 1860-70. H. 40 cm. These toys sway even when touched only slightly, because of the weights at both ends which maintain the equilibrium. Beautifully painted toys from Rajasthan, India, and amateur carved toys from Jamaica are based on the same principle.

lanesia at the end of the 19th century, fathers made models for their children of the catamarans they used for fishing. At the same time, however, they produced — for cult purposes — models of the same boats for themselves. The toy boats were usually quite simply made (for instance, a whole boat might well be carved from a single piece of wood, whereas the body of the 'model' consisted of as many separate parts as were employed to build a real ship. In toy boat models, Oceania clearly leads on a world scale; there are reports of them from practically every island in that huge region.

Among toys made primarily by adults are those employing materials derived from animals. There are camels and riders made from hippopotamus skin by certain peoples of the Sudan and Kenya; dolls and animals such as antelopes, leopards and hares moulded from dried meat covered with real fur which were familiar to the children of the Hausa of Nigeria and others of neighbouring regions. The Plains Indians made leather dolls at home, like the miniature cradles of the Lapps or the fur dolls of Siberian tribes. An unusual item is the horseback rider modelled from rubber sap in Venezuela in the 19th century.

Adults sometimes made certain technically more demanding movable toys for children, some of them very ingenious in conception and execution. Mention should be made of the 'hen' found in Turkestan, India and the United States, which was moved by a pendulum.

Amateur toymaking often existed alongside professional production. Amateur products sometimes derived from professional models, but sometimes they were quite different, or at least made from a different material. Amateur work sometimes supplemented commercial production, for example during wartime, when professional production diminished or ceased, and toys had to be made at home or not at all. In some areas, over the years, what had been a home-made toy was transformed into a commercial product oriented to the souvenir market. Similar instances of change from amateur to professional manufacture occurred as a result of the popularity of certain toys.

Although in this chapter amateur toymaking from areas outside Europe has been emphasized, amateur toys clearly dominated extensive areas of Europe. This is true especially of the Balkan peninsula, Slovakia, Spain and Portugal.

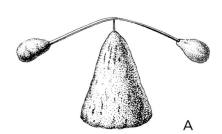

A

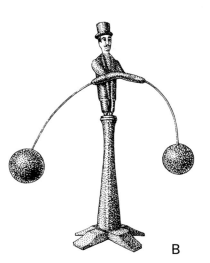

B

Professional Toymakers: Wooden Toys

Parallel with the amateur production of toys, markets in Europe and elsewhere were supplied by professional toymakers. Woodcarvers and turners sometimes depended primarily on making toys as the source of their livelihood; alternatively, they worked on toys as a secondary activity, household items being their chief business. Besides those who were specifically woodcarvers, specialists in other wood crafts for whom toymaking was a subsidiary occupation included carpenters, who in the winter months earned a living by making wooden utility objects as well as toys, cabinetmakers and coopers. Other craftsmen worked with wood in the winter season, though their main craft might be that of — for example — a mason, for whom there was less work in the winter. Production was oriented to the market and thus subject to demand.

Only a few centres — their production supplemented by smaller, local workshops — were needed to produce enough wooden toys to supply European demand. Therefore it is possible to list the names of most of the main centres or at least to describe their approximate production area. But first, something should be said about the techniques employed in these areas.

Two basic techniques are used in making wooden toys: carving and working on a lathe. Carving involves the use, normally, of small blocks of wood, though sometimes sections of whole trees. The tools were a variety of knives and chisels. In woodcarving workshops of Europe there were hundreds of chisels of different shapes. The commonest were straight chisels, with the cutting edge at right-angles to be perpendicular shaft; chisels with curved blades or V-shaped edges were also used. Similar chisels were and are used in Asia. In Africa the basic woodcarving tools are an adze and a knife, whose shapes vary according to the particular needs of local woodcarvers.

The second basic technique of making wooden toys is on a lathe, a tool independently devised in Europe, Asia and North Africa, which reached the Americas and Australia through European colonists. The simplest types are hand-powered lathes employing the bow and cord principle. To this day bow lathes are used in Yugoslavia, Greece, North Africa and in certain Asian countries, such as Iraq and India. The bowstring is wound around the wood to be turned and a horizontal movement of the body of the bow spins the wood. The movement of this type of lathe powered by a foot pedal is based on the same principle. The bow string is replaced by a cord wound around the object to be turned; one end of the rope is tied to a treadle and the other to a springy pole above the lathe, which keeps the rope tight at all times. As the treadle is pressed, the rope is pulled down; the reverse movement of the pole releases the rope, thus rotating the wood being turned. This type of lathe was used in the 19th century in the Erzgebirge region of Saxony, among many other places. The third type of lathe is based on

46 This so-called cabinet-maker's hedgehog — a wooden puzzle — came from a cabinet-maker's workshop at Valašsko (Walachia), Moravia, 1970s. One needed a certain amount of technical skill and precision to make such a puzzle and so it used to be one of the tests for apprentices. Sometimes known as the 'devil's knot'. H. 12.5 cm.

47 Figures of children, from the Erzgebirge region of Bohemia, before 1945. Their production combined the techniques of wood-turning and carving. From round, cut-off wooden sections the desired shape was turned, then cut with a knife to produce the required number of figures. These half finished products were first modelled and then painted. H. 3—4 cm.

48 Two examples of string-pulled dolls who move their arms and legs:
(A) Soldier, 19th century.
(B) Tirolean figure, 20th century.
As a rule they are soldiers, men and women in costume, or nurses with babies. Current production also includes Till Eulenspiegel figures.

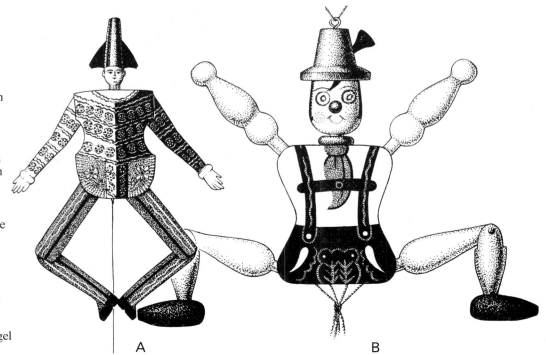

A   B

the wheel principle — the turning movement is imparted to an axle on which the wood is mounted. The invention of this type of lathe is attributed to Leonardo da Vinci (1452—1519); it was used in large European toymaking centres until the introduction of steam engines and electrical motors. Some toymakers remained faithful to the hand-turned wheel lathe well into the 20th century.

There were other types in Europe driven by water, using wooden mill wheels and a flywheel; this type was introduced to the Erzgebirge about the middle of the 18th century. Steam-driven lathes were not employed in Saxony until the second half of the 19th century. Special chisels are used to work wood turned on a lathe; their numbers run into dozens.

Apart from turned toys in the form of figures of infants, soldiers, etc., wood-carving workshops made toys requiring

47

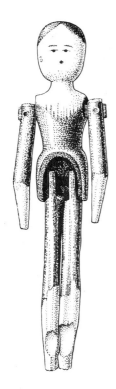

50 Wooden polychrome
doll. Val di Gardena, Italy,
19th century. The hands and
legs are movable and
fastened by pins. They are
usually sold unclothed.
H. 17 cm.

51 Baby doll in swaddling
clothes, wood with remnants
of polychrome decoration,
analogous to German 'Docke'
dolls, Bohemia, second half
of 19th century. H. 31 cm.

53 Horse rider with pendulum, wood, with part polychrome decoration. The horse and rider swing their legs. Seiffen, Germany, modern craftsmanship drawing on traditional models, 1960. H. 10 cm.

52 Crudely made wooden baby dolls can be studied from preserved examples dating back to the 16th century. Their production probably drew on an even older tradition to which, perhaps, this figure found in Usedom, Germany, and dated to the 11th century belongs.

the combined work of carving and turning. Furthermore, certain parts were made from other materials such as baked dough, various compositions of flour and glue, clay, sawdust, etc. A typical example of a combination of techniques is the method used to produce Erzgebirge animals. The basic material was wood sections cut from round timber which were then worked on a lathe. This resulted in the basic form of the animal (or other figure). The piece was then roughly sawn or carved into the shape of the required object. More detailed modelling with a knife or chisel finally produced a piece ready to be painted. Minor parts of the figure (hand, ears, tail, horns, tusks, etc. were carved or turned separately and attached before painting.

For a long time in Europe the painting of toys was separate from the actual carving or lathing and was performed by a different craftsman. The division of crafts maintained by the guilds resulted in toys being made by woodcarvers but painted by painters as late as the 18th century. The unpainted toys were transported from woodcarving centres to painting centres. Sometimes, however, the woodcarvers got around the painters' monopoly by using organic colours (from bilberries and other plants) since the painters'

54 Three-masted ship on wheels, wood and paper, probably acquired in the area of St Catherine's Mountain, Erzgebirge, Bohemia, before 1899. The same kind of ships were made in the Seiffen and Sonneberg areas. H. 20 cm, l. 20 cm.

medium was bismuthal colours, but of course the final impression was not so brilliant. Only during the 18th century did the individual toymaking centres gradually win the right to paint the finished toys with bismuth colours. In the Sonneberg area and the Alpine regions this resulted from concessions wrested from the guilds.

In the 19th century European toymaking centres began to use enamels — copal, dammar and the cheaper, poorer quality colophony resin. At the end of the 19th century the new, inexpensive aniline dyes began to take over rapidly.

With regard to the painting of toys, the situation was slightly different in Asia. The use of lacquer there is universal and has a long tradition whose roots go back at least to the first millennium B.C. The resin of different types of trees, for instance *Rhus vernicifera*, was used for lacquer; colours were added and the prepared object of paper or wood, was given several coats to produce the shiny lacquered effect. A lacquer coating protected even ordinary utility items, like bowls, dishes or wicker-baskets as well as sacred objects. It is therefore not surprising to discover that toys have lacquered surfaces. Dozens of lacquered wooden toys have survived from the 19th century; papier mâché toys were invariably lac-

55 Wooden polychrome toys from Seiffen, Germany, 19th-20th century.
(A) The angel-candleholder.
(B) The nutcracker with a Prussian helmet on its head. Nutcrackers also took the form of Turks, from Oberammergau, or young men in local costume (toymaking workshops in the Ruhr).

56 Model of a kitchen, wood with polychrome decoration. Seiffen, Germany, 1984. A modern toy based on old models. Besides kitchens, various craft workshops are also made. L. 10.7 cm, h. 3.8 cm.

quered. Although earlier mentions of Asian lacquered toys are not given in the literature, if we take the preserved items intended for other purposes, chiefly sacred dishes and carved figures, as a guide, we can assume that lacquering the surface of toys has gone on for over 2,000 years. Colourless lacquer was intended to protect the surface of toys; for instance in the territory of the former state of Savantvadi in India in the 19th century toys were painted by covering them with watercolours which were then treated two or three times with a hard, colourless coating.

In some countries of Latin America, too, especially Mexico, the use of lacquer was known in pre-Columbian times. Workshops of the colonial period took up this tradition. The spread and common use of lacquer in this part of the Americas is associated with the transfer of craft techniques through the individual possessions of the Spanish and Portuguese empires — and these were not confined to the Americas. The Philippines were a Spanish colony, the Portuguese had extensive domains in India, chiefly in Goa, as well as Indonesia and China. Among their Asian and American possessions there was lively trade and communication. In the 19th century it was quite routine in Latin American workshops to var-

nish, with colourless or coloured lacquer, the surface of toys.

On the European continent Central Europe occupied a leading position in the production of wooden toys, with producers in territories extending from the Erzgebirge of Saxony and Thuringia to Bavaria and the Tirol. This is a region rich in forests with a very old mining and woodcarving tradition. The life of miners and Central European mining culture is closely linked to woodcarving and also to the production of toys.

The history of European toymaking centres indicates that the history of wooden toys was originally closely connected with the production of sacred carving. This is true of other continents as well, where simple toymaking went hand in hand with production of the most diverse religious sculpture.

The impetus for the development of toymaking in Central Europe came through the South German towns, chiefly Augsburg, Ulm and Nuremberg. However, in the 16th and 17th centuries these cities were unable to supply the growing demands of the world market with their

own toys. It will be seen later that these 'maternal' toymaking towns not only inspired local production, but also arranged, at least at the beginning, for the marketing of the products. In all the above-mentioned towns, however, toymaking continued; for example, there were 120 workshops in Nuremberg turning out wooden toys in the mid-19th century. It is estimated that at that time, in Central European toymaking areas, 10 to 12 thousand types of toys of various kinds (and of varying quality) were produced.

In Central Europe one can point to four main toymaking centres whose history goes back at least to the 16th century. During the centuries they influenced each other with woodcarvers moving from one place to another using the same or similar models. The four centres are: the Ober-ammergau area and Berchtesgaden in Bavaria; Val di Gardena or Gröden Tal in the southern Tirol (now in Italy), the Sonneberg area of Thuringia and the Seif-fen area of Saxony. All four centres were linked by the same trading partners — the South German towns — which on the basis of demand determined the type of

▶

58   Riding school, wood and paper with polychrome decoration. Seiffen region, Germany, 1918. H. 26 cm.
Seiffen and Sonneberg catalogues from the first half of the 19th century contain a number of moving genre figures. The movement was accompanied by the sound of plucked strings hidden inside the base.

57   Seiffen toy — pigeon house with pecking hens made of wood and paper with polychrome decoration, *c.* 1898. H. 25 cm.

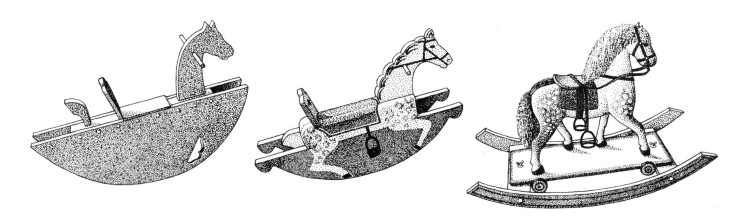

59 This developmental series of wooden rocking horses from the Eisfeld locality, Thuringia, Germany, c. 1820, 1860, 1900, demonstrates how cabinet-making products, still linked to the Baroque tradition and produced chiefly from profiled boards, changed during the 19th century into free, three-dimensional figures on rockers.

items produced. In later times, chiefly from the 19th century, the toymaking of the centres proved an inspiration to many other workshops and producers both in Europe and overseas.

In the Oberammergau area, woodcarving, particularly of sacred and secular objects, had existed as early as the 12th century; possibly the monks of the monastery at Rottenbuch were instrumental in forging this tradition. Most likely as a result of the Reformation, a break occurred in the early 16th century; production of church statues ended, to be replaced by more secular objects. After the Thirty Years' War, Oberammergau turned out painted birds, doll-rattles, dolls in swaddling clothes, soldiers, jumping-jacks, animals, miniature dishes and also a great many carved scenes from everyday life. Perhaps the toy Noah's Ark started here, although made in other Central European centres too, as well as in the workshops of Russia and

France. The wars of the 18th century had a negative effect on toymaking; probably, however, at this time there was a partial return to religious statues at Oberammergau. In the 18th and 19th centuries, production of toys continued parallel with sacred carvings, from big churches to the small personal crucifixes and little statuettes for home use, as well as Nativity figures. The manner of selling the products was the same — apart from the wholesalers who provided transportation to toy and gift shops, it was carried in the packs of house-to-house pedlars journeying across Europe. In the 19th century there was a shift from sacred carvings to decorative genre scenes, such as raftsmen or drivers with teams of animals of the kind which were hung outside public places, especially inns, as symbols of professions. Toy soldiers made in the uniform of different armies, notably Bavarian, Prussian and Turkish; figured nutcrackers, jumping-jacks, Russian wheels with four spokes (a Russian wheel of this type, from the beginning of the 20th century, has survived in Albania), teams of draught animals, dolls, and animal alphabet figures were also standard items. The Oberammergau toymakers are said to have introduced the wooden jumping-jack — the so-called Hampelmann.

The beginning of woodcarving in and around Berchtesgaden is known only from tales, which link it to the neighbouring region of Oberammergau whence, allegedly, toymaking techniques were imported. In the past two centuries, emphasis in Berchtesgaden has been on genre scenes, as documented by surviving trade catalogues and price lists. These include the barns with farm-hands, foresters, a hunter at a tree with birds, a tailor with

60 Rider on a rocking horse, wood with polychrome decoration, made famous by Seiffen and Sonneberg toymakers in the 19th and 20th centuries, although perhaps this type started in Odenwald or nearby in Hessen.

61 Two types of baby doll, wood with
polychrome decoration. Skašov, Bohemia,
before 1945. H. 20 cm and 19 cm.

62 Whistle with pinwheel, wood with polychrome decoration. When blown, the soldier 'turns' the pinwheel. Probably Klatovy, Bohemia, before 1945. L. 8 cm.

a goat, wedding carriages, etc. From Berchtesgaden come also costumed figures, painted furniture, hobby-horses and the typical horseback rider. Musical toys include barrel organs and carousels; the carvings had a thin metal plate that emitted a sound when the toy was turned round. The women of Berchtesgaden also knew how to carve wood, and children over the age of eight sometimes worked on these woodcarvings. The largest centres of production at the beginning of the 20th century were the villages of Wolkenstein and St Ulrich, the centre for the whole valley. This was where toy production was concentrated and the local middlemen bought the carvings not only from local toymakers, but also from producers in the neighbouring valleys, for instance Fassa Tal, Enneberg Tal, Villnös Tal and St Peter Tal.

Berchtesgaden toymaking influenced the development of the craft in the neighbouring Salzburg area. Following the Counter-Reformation in Bavaria, some Protestant toymakers moved to Nuremberg, thus contributing to a mingling of toy types and decorative motifs. This emigration from Berchtesgaden also encouraged the development of another toymaking centre in the Sonneberg region.

Another toymaking centre was in Gröden Valley or Val di Gardena (now in Italy), which historically belonged to Austria. For centuries Tirol toymakers co-operated with the Oberammergau region, where their products were taken to be assembled and finished. There was also close contact with producers in nearby Viehtau.

After the Thirty Years' War, when

63 Rocking horses made of plaster and wood with polychrome decoration. Uherské Hradiště, Moravia, before 1940. They resemble a type of rocking horse for which the worskhops of Seiffen and Sonneberg regions were famous. L. 8 cm.

Germany was divided and many customs barriers erected between states, the importance of South German centres such as Nuremberg declined, and their foreign-trade monopoly on toys was broken. At this time, in the 17th century and more particularly in the 18th, there was a rise in exports from Gröden Valley. The number of workshops increased from 50 to 300, and the turnover in trade rose accordingly. This was a period of prosperity for the toymaking area of Oberammergau and its dealers and agents who settled in the major ports of Western and Northern Europe. In Gröden — apart from the obligatory animals and figures — they made lathe-turned dolls with movable arms and legs. Also characteristic were the painted roosters with their bright red combs.

We have no documentation of toymaking in Sonneberg and its environs before the Thirty Years' War, but in the decades after it ended, production expanded rapidly. It seems that the prototypes or samples made in and around Berchtesgaden were given to Sonneberg carvers to copy by Nuremberg merchants. In view of the fact that in earlier periods they handled the sale of Nuremberg wooden dishes, which they brought to markets like Leipzig, they could easily have built up another partnership on this basis. However, since toymaking began to flourish only about 1700, it is more than likely that new blood was supplied by Berchtesgaden and Salzburg immigrants. There are reports, from this time, of dolls in swaddling bands known as *Docken*, of countrywomen churning butter, of horse-riders and pinwheels. From a later period there are figures of miners, nutcrackers, birds and boats with sailors. Rocking horses, whistles, fiddles, swords, rifles, tops, and 'singing' birds were made by employment of the principles of bellows and whistle. During the 18th century the production began of dolls made of materials other than wood, for instance of wax and plaster, and after 1806 production of papier mâché dolls was launched on a large scale. However, the production of wooden toys persisted into the 20th century.

The first mention of carvers from Seiffen and its environs comes from the end of the Middle Ages. There is reference to the existence of the carvers' craft in the 15th century, when wooden-turned dishes were made at Seiffen. Seventeenth-century reports give more precise details about lathe-turned dishes and spindles, which

64   Porcelain jar with the motif of festive procession with children carrying a kite. China, 1644-1912. The jar must be turned around so that the viewer sees the whole procession. This method of painting a procession is derived from the Chinese horizontal scroll, seen as it gradually unfolded. H. 22 cm, d. bottom 14.4 cm.

were sold at Leipzig's fairs. In the 17th century there was another shift in production: besides dishes and other utility objects, toys began to be made, lathe-turned and carved. A description of the production of lathe-profiled sections from which miniature animal figures were cut suggests that the technical methods employed were similar to those used in producing turned dishes. In the 16th century, if not

earlier, figures of miners were modelled and carved in the Seiffen district, so it is likely that the toymaking tradition is much older there than records can prove. The fact that during the Thirty Years' War Protestant immigrants from Bohemia settled here must have played a role in these developments in the Seiffen area.

If the 17th century was a period of preparation in the Seiffen area, then the 18th

65 Miniature village with domestic and
exotic animals, wood with polychrome
decoration. Erzgebirge, before 1978. In these
parts toys were turned on a lathe from the
17th century, but only *c.* 1814 did one of the
Seiffen masters invent a new approach:
turning profiled rings from which the figures
were then cut. H. houses 4 cm, trees
4.5 cm, animals 2.5 cm.

66   A figure probably
representing an officer,
wood with polychrome
decoration.
Tirolean-Bavarian region,
c. first half of 19th century.

67   Rooster or peacock on wheels, wood
with polychrome decoration. Val di
Gardena, Italy, before 1941. H. 11.5 cm.

century, when mining declined, witnessed
the full glory of toymaking and woodcarving production. Its development can be
followed through records of the increasing number of woodcarving lathes in Seiffen and environs. In 1644 there was one;
in 1670, 23; in 1770, 100; in 1870, 675.
At the beginning of the 20th century the
people of about 50 settlements and villages were engaged in this work. During
the 18th and 19th centuries production
was not confined only to the Saxon part of
the Erzgebirge, but returned once again to
the Czech side of the range, where St

Catherine's Mountain (Katharinaberg)
became one of the main centres, as did
nearby villages, with Litvínov and Kalich
in the lead.

About the end of the 19th or beginning
of the 20th century certain villages in the
Seiffen district began to specialize. Hall-
bach became famous for its Noah's Ark
with animals, which was also made in Oberammergau. In Obernau the specialities
were little houses, dishes and riders on
rocking horses. In Rothenthal it was skit-
tles and chessmen, in Deutschendorf
boxes and pen-cases, in Deutscheinsiedel

68   Clapper in the form of turning dolls, wood with polychrome decoration. Bought at a market in Klatovy, Bohemia, before 1939. Similar clappers appeared with printed patterns in Val di Gardena in the 19th century. H. 23.5 cm.

69   Miniature rack wagon and mail coach, both with draught animals, wood with polychrome decoration. Seiffen, Germany, before 1961. Example of miniature toys from the Erzgebirge. H. wagons 3.5 cm, l. 10.5 cm and 8.5 cm.

70 Examples of genre figures made in Skašov, Bohemia, wood with polychrome decoration. Peasant woman churning butter, mother with child, and hussar, before 1945. H. hussar 17,3 cm, mother 19.5 cm, peasant woman 18.5 cm.

71   Military bugler on a horse, wood with
polychrome decoration. Skašov, Bohemia,
first quarter of the 20th century. This
workshop made hussars and dragoons with
swords, and buglers and infantrymen with
swords or rifles. H. 25 cm, l. 19.5 cm.

72 Pull-along cart with roundabouts bearing figures of horses, wood with polychrome decoration. Poland, before 1961. Pull-carts built on the same principle are found in Russia and the Tirol. H. 15 cm, l. 22 cm.

forest animals of several kinds, in Oberseiffenbach jumping-jacks, in Heidelberg a marketplace full of people, and in Blumenau building bricks.

Similar local specialization occurred in the Sonneberg district and other villages of Thuringia, and must certainly have existed even in Bavaria and Tirolean centres. In the Sonneberg district, the village of Mangersgereuth-Hämmern specialized in making little ships. Other Thuringian villages — for instance, Friedrichroda, Finsterbergen, Georgenthal and Waltershausen — specialized in jointed dolls.

Among recent Seiffen specialities are nutcrackers, pipe-smokers and torchbearers. The figure of a nutcracker as a magic puppet was made famous in Tchaikovsky's ballet, based on a story by Alexandre Dumas, which in turn derived from

73 Whistle in the form of a bird, wood with polychrome decoration. Slovakia, before 1926. Ordinary whistles of hazel wood were made for the annual open-air fairs. They sold so quickly that it paid to build up a supply for the one fair day of the year. H. 12 cm.

74 Wooden polychrome figures 'walking' down along an incline. All were made on the Czech side of the Bohemian Forest (these shown here in Chlum near Hartmanice) in the 1920s and exported to Australia and England. 'Walking' figures of St Nicholas, black nannies, and peasant women were also made.
(A) Man in top hat. H. 12.5 cm.
(B) Monkey. H. 11 cm.
(C) Dog. H. 11 cm.
(D) Elephant. H. 9 cm, l. 12 cm.

fairytales in which the figure of the nutcracker appeared. The German author, artist and musician E. T. A. Hoffmann, published a fairytale in 1816, *The Nutcracker and the Mouse King*. It would seem that in the Seiffen district the nutcracker is a fairly new toy, first being made there by the carver Wilhelm Füchtner (1844—1923). It was his son who introduced the popular smoker — genre figures whose mouths or pipes emitted smoke, and torchbearers. The figure-type nutcracker, who cracks nuts in his mouth, is older — dating from the first half of the 18th century. It was also produced in Sonneberg, where it appears at the end of the 18th century in a list of items offered for sale at the Leipzig fairs as a boys' toy. Such items were also made in Gröden, Oberammergau and Berchtesgaden.

 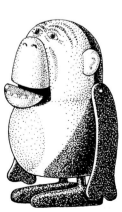  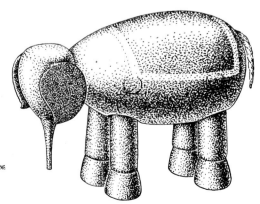

A   B   C   D

75 A pull-along cart with two rotating birds. It was acquired in Russia in 1941 but is most likely to be a Polish or Ukrainian import. H. 20 cm, w. 17 cm.

76 Makers of the Russian *matrëshka* (nest of dolls) drew on the history and ethnic composition of the population, and so there are sets of Russian heroes or women in national costume. Lathe turner V. Zvëzdochkin and painter S. Malyutin were among the pioneers of these figures in the 1890s.

77 Samovar, painted
wood. Yaroslavl district,
Russia, before 1901.
Sometimes inside the
samovar there were
miniature dishes for making
and drinking tea. H. 19 cm,
d. 7.5 cm.

In the Erzgebirge, the use of nutcrackers and torchbearers in the form of miners or angels carrying candles was associated with the Advent period, when the same number of nutcrackers or miners as the number of sons in a family was placed on the window sill, while the number of angels on the sill corresponded to the number of girls in the family. This custom persists to the present day.

Since the 19th century, miniature wooden kitchens, rooms and tiny workshops have been made in the Erzgebirge region. Their appearance draws on a far older tradition of miniaturizing fully furnished houses, intended both for the pleasure of adults and as a plaything for children. Their beginnings can be traced to the second half of the 16th century, the oldest mention of houses being from between 1558 and 1599. A picture of them has survived from 1631 and reports of the manufacture of these two-storeyed houses with four rooms dates from 1673. The centre of trade in these houses was Nuremberg — the inspirational source al-

so of Erzgebirge wooden toys, so it is most probably to Nuremberg that one should look for the origin of the little wooden rooms and houses that even today are made at Seiffen and elsewhere.

There are various types of Erzgebirge movable toys, powered either by a windmill, which is blown, or turned by a stream of warm air, or by winding up a crank. The windmills date mainly from a period around 1700. Sometimes several tiers of riding schools, miners' parades, etc. were attached to the common axle of a windmill or carousel. Larger examples of these windmills are linked to Advent. The crank-type carousels probably came into existence about the beginning of the 19th century.

An Erzgebirge speciality associated with mining tradition is the figure of a miner in the form of, typically, a candle-holder, besides whole parades of miners. Sets including a whole mining town together with figures of miners at work were also produced. The figures are dressed in Sunday-best clothes, even though they are

78   Horses, wood with polychrome decoration, from around Lake Siljan, Dalarna district, Sweden, before 1938. These horses are red, blue, black and white; however, the most popular and also best known are the red horses. They come in different sizes — from half a metre to a few centimetres. H. 14.5 cm.

79 Cradle, wood.
Sarajevo, Bosnia and
Herzegovina, before 1901.
H. 21 cm, 1. 30 cm.

digging a tunnel, crushing coal or pushing wagons. There are examples in tin as well as wood.

Large toys such as rocking horses were produced in all centres. Their type changed in the course of the 19th century, as can be seen by tracing three examples from Eisfeld, in the Sonneberg district. The oldest phase is that of the baroque rocking horse, known also in the 17th century in England, in which the horse's head protrudes from a plank-sided body. In the next phase the support element has painted horse's legs, and in the third phase the whole body of the horse appears with individually cut legs.

Several toymaking centres of smaller size made their reputations by imitating models of wooden toys produced in the larger European centres. Their products supplied, perhaps, only one country or part of it, though in certain cases they contributed to the exports of the main toymaking centres.

Because Central European toys travelled across continents and passed through the hands of middlemen of different nationalities, they are known under different names. In England they were known as Dutch dolls, not because they were made in the Netherlands (though that may have been the belief of English customers), but because they were imported from Dutch ports. Similarly, moving hens that pecked, as at corn, were often attributed to Slovakia because they

80 Wooden polychrome
doll from Italy with
movable arms, 17th century.

81 Wooden doll from
Narainpur village, Medinipur
district, Bengal, India, 1976.
This stylized woman's figure
is carved from wood (a stick).
H. 22 cm, w. 5.5 cm.

82 Tiger, wood with polychrome decoration. Puri, Orissa state, India, before 1967. Figures of elephants are also popular. Toys in this style are taken from famous Puri paintings. H. 15.8 cm and 12.8 cm.

were distributed from the workshops in Bohemia and Bavaria by Slovak pedlars.

Competition from the big Central European centres was often too heavy for the local workshops because of the former's high standards of production and relatively low prices. The situation in England serves as an example. Wooden soldiers were exported to England and were very popular around the mid-19th century. Their uniforms were painted in the manner of British regiments (naturally, manufacturers took the tastes and

wishes of customers into account). This practice was commonplace in all the big centres and also in centres working for bigger exporters; for example, in Hlinsko in Bohemia, 'Tirolean' dolls were exported to the Tirol. Not until the 1880s did the native British toymaking industry begin to develop on a large scale in London workshops.

In Denmark the situation was much the same, but there local production began to compete successfully with foreign imports only at the end of the 19th century. From *c.* 1900 one finds wooden, painted jumping-jacks representing Danish Guards. Dolls without clothes were exported to Finland in the 19th century: customers sewed clothes for the dolls at home. In Österbotten there was local production of wooden dolls, but it was constantly fighting foreign competition.

In Germany, too, some of the old toy-making centres were unable to keep up with the competition from the larger, more up-to-date centres, and in the 19th century their production was restricted to local markets only. This was the case, for instance, in the Odenwald district of Hesse. The popular toy riders on hobby horses, which probably began production in Niederhausen around the mid-19th century, are attributed to the toymakers of the Odenwald district. A. Spamer, the author of a work on folk art in Hesse, notes that this Odenwald horse became famous only when it was produced in the Sonneberg and Seiffen districts, whence it was exported all over the world. In the Odenwald district, too, little wagons, hobby-horses and horse-drawn carts were made for children.

Small woodwork shops also existed in Augsburg and the surrounding area in the 19th century. Local toymaking work-shops in Switzerland, for example in Berne, and in Austria remained in the shadow of the major centres.

In the Czech lands there were three large centres and a number of smaller ones, the latter situated in the border regions. Among the big toymaking centres of the interior, the greatest was the village of Skašov in central Bohemia, where the roots of production go back to the time of the Napoleonic Wars. After a railway was built, Skašov products were exported to the whole of what was then the Austro-Hungarian Empire and also to other countries, including North America. In 1913 a toymaking co-operative was established there which marketed its own products and was less dependent on middle-men. Besides dolls in swaddling bands, they made genre figures of people, horse-back riders, horses, wagons with teams of horses, birds, whistles and rattles, guns, dishes, pinwheels and moving snakes. A similar assortment was brought out in another centre, Hlinsko and its environs,

83　Jacob's ladder: made of coloured wood and fabric, by tipping the upper block to the right or left the toy is set in motion and the individual blocks keep moving. Catalonia, Spain, 1970s. Blocks 6 × 6 cm.

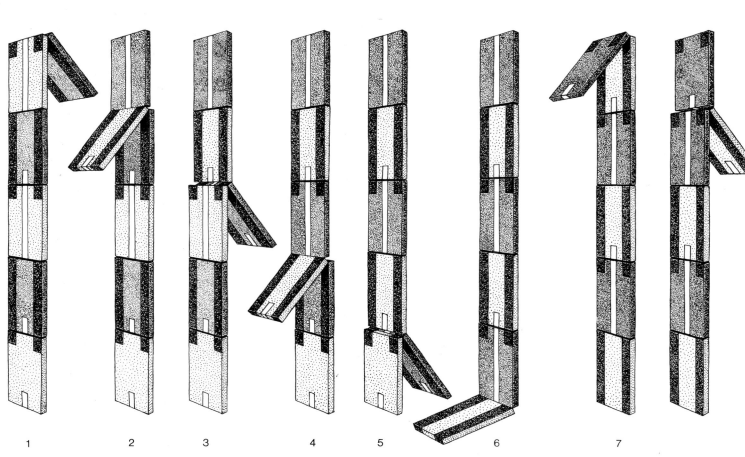

1　　2　　3　　4　　5　　6　　7

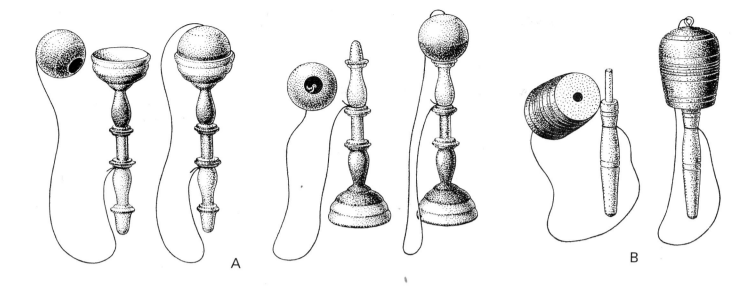

A   B

84 The home of bilboquets (cup and ball) is, perhaps, North America, where they entertained both Indians and Eskimos, but they were used in ancient times. In the 16th century they were widespread in France and from there they reached England. They were among the most popular playthings even in the 19th century. The toy from Savantvadi district, India, has a ball which can be caught either in a cup or on a 'needle', 1870s (A). The second example was made in Mexico before 1982 (B). Both are of polychrome wood. H. 21 cm.

especially the village of Krouná where production lasted longest.

The history of the third major Czech toymaking centre — Příbram and the surrounding villages — is linked to mining and mineral extraction. Toys were produced there in the 18th century, Příbram being an important pilgrimage site where such items enjoyed good sales. The greatest period of toymaking, however, was from 1885 to 1916. Fifty-two families in Příbram itself and 53 families in nearby villages earned a living producing toys. Apart from figures of soldiers, infants, mother and child, and miners, they made a great variety of genre figures: watchmen, laundresses, tinkers, cobblers at work. They also produced genre scenes, such as processions at funerals. Nativity scenes including figures of the visitors to the stable at Bethlehem were made which resembled the toy figures, and for the St Nicholas market (December 6) they produced wooden devils. Moving toys too were part of their production programme; some were based on the swing or pendulum principle.

In Králíky, and its surroundings in eastern Bohemia, toys were sometimes carved from semifinished boards and sometimes turned. Here too the production of Nativity scenes merged with toymaking. In the foothills of the Riesengebirge (Krkonoše), a region of many folk tales, carvers drew on folklore traditions and the craft of the *objet trouvé* in figures of Krakonoš, the lord of these mountains, which were made of suitable sticks. On the Czech side of the Erzgebirge, there were two larger centres.

One was the area of Katharinaberg, Litvínov, Kalich and surrounding villages; the second was the town of Kraslice and its environs. Toys from the former were similar to those made in Seiffen while in Kraslice the producers also specialized in musical toys. There were a number of workshops in the Bohemian Forest (Šumava), such as Domažlice in the Tachov district and Vacov near Klatovy, but these were mainly turners' shops producing toys only as secondary products. Some of them were associated with other woodworking enterprises, such as the local sawmill. In addition to the usual types, at the beginning of the 20th century they produced toys that moved down a slope, similar to those from the Seiffen area.

There were other small workshops in Moravia and Slovakia and on the Moravian side of the Beskydy Mountains. However, the toymaking tradition there is relatively new. In Valašsko (Walachia), around Valašská Bystřice and the neighbouring villages of northern Moravia, toys were made of smoked beechwood engraved with decoration, which were instantly successful when first produced at the end of the 19th century. Wheelbarrows and wooden dishes were popular items in this medium.

In Slovakia in the second half of the 19th and the 20th centuries there were several centres. These included the workshop in Piarg (today's Štiavnická Baňa), which made animals, houses and carriages based on Tirolean and Salzburg models. Another centre was the village of Kunešov, inhabited by German settlers.

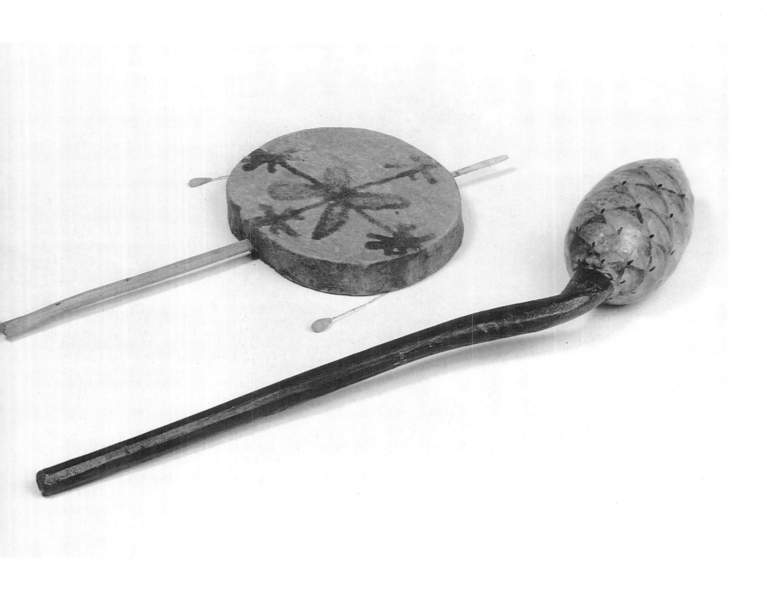

85 Two musical toys:
a clapper-drum, recalling the
drums of the Lamaist region,
and a rattle in the form of
a pine cone. They are of
wood and leather with
polychrome decoration and
lacquer. The rattle is of
unknown origin, the drum
from Orissa, India, before
1878. L. rattle 39.5 cm,
drum 30.4 cm, d. drum
13.2 cm.

There the specialities were animal figures
painted with oil colours and figures of
little red deer. In Stará Turá they made
pecking hens, whose production was at its
greatest in the first half of the 20th century. In Kyjatice toys were made from
stained wood decorated with engraved
patterns. The toys were based on the local
production of cabinets and chests and so,
apart from children's carts and wagons,
miniature furniture formed a substantial
proportion of output. Toymaking in
Spišská Belá has a unique history: after
the opening of the railway to the Tatra
Mountains, the demand for souvenirs increased. At first they were shipped from
the Berchtesgaden area of Bavaria, and
only at the end of the 19th century were
souvenirs and toys produced locally. Toys
made in neighbouring areas of Poland
were also sold here.

In Poland toymaking declined in the
first half of the 20th century, but after the
Second World War it was given new impetus through the efforts of the Polish
state to preserve folk culture. Thanks to
this help, many amateur woodcarvers
now create wooden toys and sculptural
pieces drawing on old models and based
on traditional values. Thus one finds at
markets in Nowy Targ and Rzeszów, as
well as in other cities, hobby-horses, cradles, hay barrows, figures of people and
animals, or birds that run on wheels. The
centre of toymaking was and remains
Galicia, an area rich in timber and famous
in other spheres of folk woodcarving.
Among other traditional Polish centres
are Koszarawa, Lachowice, Łączna, Os-
trojew, Brzoza Stawnicka and Poręba. Lachowice itself and the villages in the vicin-
ity supplied toys to the whole of Poland.

86 Model of a hand-mill and rattle, wood with polychrome decoration. Savantvadi district, India, before 1878. Mill d. 14.6 cm, h. 16.4 cm.

Toymakers in the town itself specialized in bird figures; in the area around the town they made horses, pull-along wagons with moving figures of horses or birds, cradles, birds and butterflies on wheels that flap their wings when pulled along.

The development of toymaking in Poland was essentially similar to that of other European centres. For example, in Brzoza Stawnicka carvers originally made full-sized wooden dishes, but with the arrival of factory-made products, local production ceased and toymaking provided a way out of this crisis. At the end of the 19th century, most of the master crafts-men there made horses, then often unpainted; only during the 20th century was painting added. In the 1930s, in all Polish toymaking centres, the traditional assortment was expanded to include such movable toys as birds pulled on wheels, hens pecking for seed, etc. After the Second World War they began to make toys in the shape of motor vehicles and other modern means of transport.

Besides professional woodcarvers, stonecutters played an important role in Polish toymaking. In the Cracow area, during the winter season, they made rattles, decorative miniature axes and figures

87 Doll, wood with
polychrome decoration.
Japan, before 1961. Lathe-
turned puppets known as
kokeshi are among the best
known Japanese folk toys,
and are still being made.
H. 24 cm.

88 The tiger and the yearling *shika* (which means yearling in Japanese) are modern, 20th-century Japanese toys (before 1925). This can be seen from the rockers on which the animals stand. L. 13.5 cm, h. *c.* 10.5 cm.

of people in local costume. Lęczyca stonecutters produced wooden birds and sheep for the Easter markets.

The toymaking tradition of the Lvov area (now in the western Ukraine) is connected with the woodcarving tradition of the Galicia area which in the past was an important production centre of wooden toys. Besides Lvov, wooden toys were made chiefly in nearby Yavorov. There are some documented examples of wooden rattles, painted carriages, clarinets, lathe-turned globes, and figures of animals from the last quarter of the 19th century. The Khmel'nitsko area of the Ukraine made, among others, toys that emitted sounds, produced by saw-edges, etc.

Along the Baltic, in Lithuania and Latvia, there are popular fairy-tales about devils. The devils not only punished sinners, but also played pranks on people, both good and bad. Figures of them are popular toys in Kaunas in Lithuania, which has a museum devoted to devils. In the other Baltic countries these wooden figures of

toy devils sometimes took the form of nutcrackers.

In Russia there were toymaking centres in and around Moscow, for example Zagorsk (formerly Sergiev Posad) and Bogorodskoe, whose proximity to a big city, plus the presence of visitors to pilgrimage sites in Zagorsk, provided a healthy market. In Zagorsk, wooden toys are recorded in the 17th century and contemporary reports speak of serfs of the Troitsky Monastery carving toys in Sergiev Posad and other neighbouring villages. During the 17th century, members of the Tsar's family bought toys here. A report from 1721 lists toys bought in Moscow, but made in Zagorsk. It mentions figures of cows, horses, deer, sheep, and pairs of swans, roosters, ducks with three ducklings, a town with soldiers, and carriages. Characteristic of Zagorsk toymaking in the 19th century were wooden figures of ladies and hussars, carved from sticks. The carvers here were also inspired by world events: after the War of 1812 they began making soldiers; around 1877, af-

89 A puppet used as
a toy and an amulet. It was
brought from Bijogo, the
Bissagos Islands, in the
1920s. Its traditional use has
persisted to this day.
H. 71.3 cm.

Later, the local toymakers produced the finished toy, though it was still sent to Zagorsk to be painted. Only during the 19th century did the Bogorodskoe toymakers become fully independent. Co-operation between Zagorsk and Bogorodskoe was simple since the two places are only 22 kilometres apart.

In the Gorky area, there were several centres with toymaking traditions of varying age. Besides the workshops in the city itself, there were others in existence in the Semenov district as early as the 17th century. In the town of Lyskovo they made dolls, among other items, but the woodcarvers there were famous chiefly for their horses. Figures were carved or turned and, depending on local conditions, the wood used was lime, alder, ash and birch. Another centre in the same district was the town of Gorodtse, but there toymaking began only in the 1890s. In the village of Babenki, in the Moscow area, there was intensive toy production prior to the First World War. Other workshops were located in and around the cities of Vologda and Yaroslavl.

In the Urals, woodcarving and toymaking traditions go back to the 18th century. The objects most often associated with this area are dishes and wooden boxes of infinite variety, painted with brightly coloured flowers. Toys, which were secondary products, were shipped as far away as Central Asia. The main Urals production centres were the towns of Nizhni Tagil and Nenyansk.

In addition to Russians themselves, the Russian empire contained many toymakers of other nationalities. The Komi-Ziryan people turned out the usual types of Russian wooden toys, such as horses on wheels and *matrëshkas* (nests of wooden dolls with Asiatic faces). These toys were sold throughout the Russian empire and many found their way abroad.

Apart from wooden human figures and horses, Russia is known for its characteristic *troika*, three horses harnessed abreast to a carriage, its genre scenes of dancers, and historical figures, Napoleon and others. There are countless carved genre scenes from village life, of sowing and harrowing the fields, herding sheep, and hunting scenes. Quite common are figures of famous generals, musicians, monks and nuns. Biblical subjects appear, notably Noah's Ark, Jonah and the whale and

ter the Turkish war, they produced figures of Russian soldiers at whose foot sat a small Turkish soldier. Workshops in Zagorsk probably influenced toymaking in Vladimir and Gorky (Nizhni Novgorod).

In the Vladimir district, the centre was the village of Bogorodskoe. Originally, some of the toys were merely carved there and sent onto Zagorsk to be finished.

78

90 Rooster and quail, painted wood. Japan, before 1925. Rooster h. 7.2 cm, quail h. 4 cm, l. 8 cm.

King Solomon delivering his judgement. At the end of the 19th century and in the early 20th toys parodying the tsarist autocracy appeared though they were somewhat restricted.

A pair of blacksmiths, or a blacksmith and a bear hammering on an anvil, was a popular mechanical toy. Bears in fact were very versatile in the hands of the toymakers. They act as nannies, dancers, or chimney sweeps; they pump water, sail a boat, step on a hedgehog; there are even examples of a bears' wedding.

The mechanical toy with two blacksmiths hammering on an anvil probably spread to Siberia through Russian colonization. They are known in other parts of Europe, however, for instance in Poland and Bohemia, and there is an Egyptian variant from the end of the 19th century. The first toys using this mechanical principle date from the first half of the 19th century.

The figure of the bear is also known as a non-mobile toy, frequently in combination with a trainer: together they play on musical instruments, stroll side by side, or accompany each other in a dance.

A classic modern Russian folk toy is the turned nest of hollow dolls of ascending size, the *matrëshka*, which fit into each other. They are usually figures of women but were also made in combination with the figure of Grandfather Frost. The individual figures, each smaller than the next, may differ from one another in the colour of their clothes, although the overall decoration, either painted or pokerwork, is the same for the whole set. They have existed in this form only since the 1890s and their roots should be sought in the Far East. They are, in fact, offshoots of the Japanese *Daruma* figures, which also appear sometimes as dolls' nests, one fitting into another. But miniature toys that fit into one another, such as mushrooms

91 Emperor and empress, wood with polychrome decoration. Japan, before 1945. Although there are more figures in the set, those of the royal pair are essential; if other figures are missing then at least two lanterns are used. The oldest reference to children's rooms and dolls known as *hina* are from the beginning of the 11th century. H. 6.5 cm and 8.5 cm, d. 9.5 cm.

92 Dolls made of stained wood. Mossi tribe, Burkina Faso, 20th century. H. *c.* 20 cm.

containing turned dishes, or samovars holding implements for making tea, were great favourites in Russia and seem to have appealed to Russian woodcarvers.

Wooden toys decorated with big flowers come from the Urals region and north-ern Russia and also appear in Scandinavia, perhaps having the same cultural roots. Among the best-known Swedish toys are horses and roosters painted with flowers against a red, white or yellow background. They were made in and around Stockholm, also in Kopparbergs Län (formerly the Dalarna district). Toymaking once again appears in association with mining in Sweden. In the territory of Kopparberg ('Copper Mountain'), where from about the 11th century iron ore and non-ferrous metals were mined, ponies were bred to work in the mines. They were, most probably, the inspiration for the toy ponies of the region, and their red colouring, often used on toys, was obtained as a subsidiary product of ore extraction. The tradition of depicting horses goes back to the 16th century, although they then appeared only on votive and commemorative pictures. Production of

80

93   Unit of Russian soldiers which turn
right and left as the wooden pantograph is
moved. Wood with polychrome decoration,
before 1896. L. 47 cm, h. 14 cm. Toys made
in Russian and German workshops are found
representing units of hussars, musicians or
flocks of sheep with shepherds.

94   Two smiths and an anvil — mechanical
toy, wood with polychrome decoration.
Russia, before 1896. The figures of the
smiths are a triangular cross-section, of
a block of wood. L. 27.5 cm, h. 11 cm.

95   Rooster, wood with polychrome
decoration, from around Lake Siljan,
Kopparbergs Län, Sweden, before 1938.
H. 10.5 cm.

96 Dolls, wood and pulp with polychrome
decoration. Western Bengal, India, before
1962. The larger doll is carved from wood,
the smaller is made of tree pulp. H. 19 cm
and 13.7 cm.

97   Milkseller with his wares, wood and
papier mâché with polychrome decoration.
Madras, India, before 1955. Replica of
a traditional genre figure from Kondapalli,
drawing on subjects that are part of
India's past. H. 9 cm, base 12.8 × 11.3 cm.

98 Camel and elephant, wood with polychrome decoration. Jaipur, Rajasthan, India, before 1878. Before painting, the figures were coated with a mixture of grey-white clay and water; after drying, this base was then smoothed and polished. The white clay was made by pulverizing soft stone. After painting, the figures were lacquered. H. 15.2 cm and 17.6 cm.

99   Ink pot in the shape of a carved
peacock with figures of girls, wood with
polychrome decoration. Udaipur, India,
before 1958. This is a traditional gift that
sisters gave their brothers as a mark of
respect. H. 26.3 cm, l. 26 cm.

100   Cart with a team of oxen, painted
plywood. Wherever two-wheeled carts are
used one also finds miniatures as
playthings. Rangoon, Burma, before 1969.
They are also common in Benares, India, and
in Portugal and Sicily.

101 Doll, wood with
polychrome decoration,
paint on clay. Kanuri,
Nigeria, 1974. The stylized
figure without hands follows
the traditional way of
simplifying toys, leading
to three-legged camels
and horses. H. 25 cm.

wooden horses and other animals is documented from the 18th century, when mining began to decline. At the present time, toymaking still continues in about five villages near Lake Siljan, the best known of which is Nussnäs. Miniature cows, roosters and various birds are carved, in addition to horses.

In Norway the tradition of making wooden horseback riders on wheels can be traced from the 17th century. In the 19th century figures of red-painted horses were made in Hallingdal and other places, also horseback riders accompanied by a dog.

An important toymaking centre in France was Notre-Dame-de-Liesse, Aisne, where wagons, furniture, turned dolls and riders, whistles in the from of roosters, pinwheels and boats on wheels were made. The style of these toys recalls the products of Central European workshops. In Arles, in southern France, miniature models of craftsmen's workshops, including individual rooms, were made. From southern France also came wooden and painted animals on wheels, such as lions, roosters and pheasants. Among musical instruments there were clappers combined with whistles, looking somewhat like castanets — their surface varnished after being painted. Noah's Arks

102 Stylized dolls, painted wood. Yoruba, Nigeria, before 1968. Toys that girls play with become amulets when they come of age. H. 20.8 cm, 10.4 cm and 17.5 cm.

103 Doll of wood with
polychrome decoration from
Ibo or Ibibio, Nigeria, before
1967. In addition to
female figures, genre
scenes are also found.
H. 25.5 cm.

104 Doll of stained wood, signed 'Hamba of Shamusengo'. Kuba, Kahemba region, Zaire, before 1949. The figure wears a typical Kuba cap on its head. An item housed in the British Museum, London, documenting the use of such dolls from the beginning of the 20th century. H. 21 cm.

with multicoloured straw roofs were also made there.

In Italy most toymaking workshops were to be found in the southern part of the peninsula, in the provinces of Lucania and Calabria, and in Sicily. Sicilian toymaking was concentrated in the towns of Syracuse, where musical toys were made,

and Palermo, where miniature Sicilian carts were produced. Sicilian carvers also made wooden marionettes for puppet plays. Toymaking workshops produced lacquered animals, models of ships and carts (Rome), movable painted toys (Turin) and marionettes (Florence). The big toymaking centre that has already been

105 Doll made of raffia
palm pulp and hammered
bark. Ubangi-Shari River
basin, Zaire, before 1949.
Also found in the
Cameroons, for instance
among the Bafia; sometimes
they come in pairs and when
pulled by a string they jump.
H. 16.5 cm, max. w. 9.5 cm.

  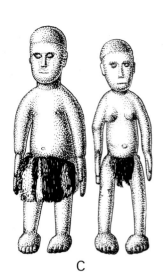

A   B   C

106 These south African wooden dolls from the beginning of the 20th century, partly stained, are a rare example of figure woodcarving in those parts. Examples are from:
(A) Chopi tribe,
(B) Gwamba tribe,
(C) Venda tribe.

107 Figure of elephant, wood with burned pattern and staining. Luba, Zaire, before 1966. H. 15 cm, l. 28 cm.

mentioned, in the Gröden Valley (Val di Gardena) in northern Italy, was able to saturate most of Italy with its toys. But south of these, in Lombardy, was another such centre. A large concentration of workshops in Milan produced work in which the influence of Central Europe is plainly evident.

In south-eastern Europe, besides lathe-turned toys, carved toys were produced in sets, chiefly two- and three-note whistles shaped like birds, from Slovenia. They were usually decorated with simple painting. From Greece there are small wooden figures of horses, dogs and birds, and toys drawing on local folklore, such as a movable toy circus artiste on a trapeze, who looks like the folk hero Karankiores. Apart from purely local items, products similar to those of the Central European centres also found a market here, but it is not entirely certain whether they were locally made or imported. Also from Greece came birds on wheels whose wings flap as they are pulled, while in Croatia there were wagons with carousels on which costumed dancers performed. In Bulgaria mechanical toys using the pen-

108 So-called big (Russian) wheel made of plywood. This toy was produced in Mexico before 1982. H. 40 cm.

dulum principle — a man with a donkey or a fish — were popular.

Wooden whistles in the shape of birds, sticks used in ball games, Catalan mechanical toys of the type known as Jacob's ladder, and spinning tops represent the bulk of Spanish toymaking. Their development came about only towards the end of the 19th century when they began to hold their own against Central European competition.

Miniature musical instruments were made in all European countries; their shape derived from real instruments, differing little except for the painted decoration which is a clue to their origin. Tiny

Russian fiddles have large flower motifs of the kind found on Russian wagons. Little flutes, clarinets, trumpets and drums were also made. Wooden whistles, some in the shape of birds, are to be found throughout Europe and probably derived from one of the most widespread ceramic toys — the figural whistle. These one-, two- or three-tone whistling birds were represented both in the production of big Central European centres and among products of local workshops.

In the Indian subcontinent (including what are now Pakistan, Bangladesh and other countries), countless workshops were devoted to carving wooden toys and

95

110 Papoose for a doll, wood with relief carving, fabric, embroidered with porcupine quills. Eastern Dakotas, U.S.A., before 1867. Inside the papoose is a quilt; the embroidery probably depicts dogs. L. 42 cm, w. 21 cm.

◄
109 *Kachina* — a wood-carving depicting two dancers wearing ghost masks. It was acquired before 1893 from New Mexico, U.S.A., and its owner wrote: '*Kachina* is the protective little god of the Indian Hopi tribe. The Indian Hopi now give idols to children as toys.' H. 27.8 cm, w. 21.5 cm.

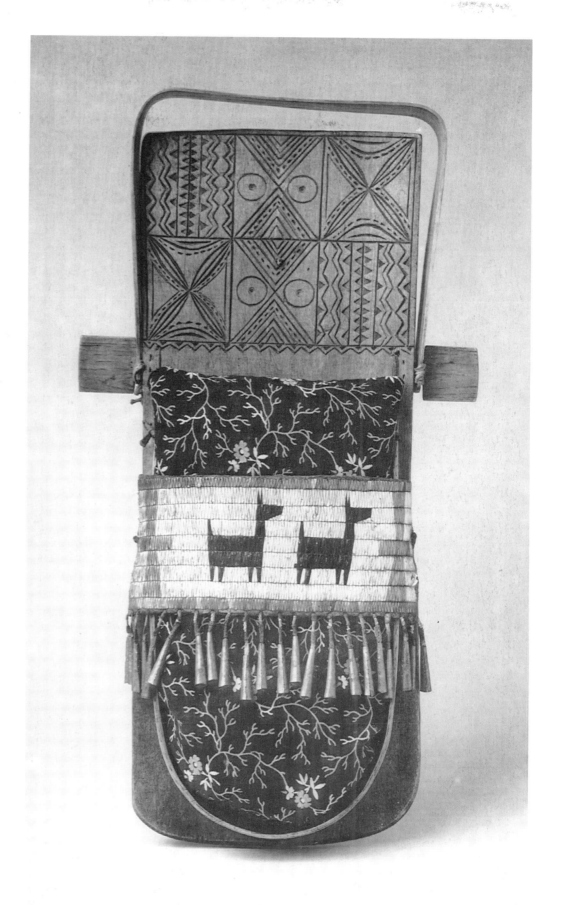

the variety of their products is equally great. As mentioned earlier, apart from ordinary timber, toys were made from the softer material of certain trees and plants. Hindu producers are members of a special sub-caste of carpenters, *sutradharas*, and toys are one of their auxiliary products. Part of the work is done by people of the lowest caste, the so-called Untouchables. Besides toys equally familiar in Europe, such as animals, dishes, musical instruments, carts and rattles, Indian craftsmen made many figures of gods which were not only playthings but were also intended to protect children. In Bengal these often take the form of Kartik, the god of war, or of Rama, his wife Sita and his brother Lakshman. Images of the god Vishnu (Jagannath) and his siblings, his sister Subhadra and brother Balarama, also come from Bengal. Relatives buy children miniature copies of temple wagons carrying figures of these gods in the processions which take place incorporating life-sized temple wagons. The little wagons containing figures of gods are among the most popular toys in this part of India.

Insofar as techniques are concerned, the making of Indian toys does not differ from European practice. Once again they are turned on a lathe and carved by hand, painted in bright colours and varnished, or left unpainted. Lacquer was used much more extensively than in Europe and in a number of centres wooden toys are given a plaster coating before being painted.

A role in protecting traditional Indian toymaking was played by the British colonial administration in the 19th century which, by supporting local handicrafts, hoped to provide a living for people who would otherwise be unemployed. Toys, at least those from favoured centres, appeared at exhibitions and were also sold as souvenirs. After India became independent, similarly protective measures were imposed by the national and state governments. In the 1950s and 1960s, there were still dozens of workshops in the Republic of India, scattered throughout the country and grouped around larger toymaking centres. Monographs on the folk art of India increasingly report on folk toymaking.

111   Lorry, wood with polychrome decoration. Mexico, before 1982. L. 68 cm, h. 24.5 cm.

112 Easter rattles, wood with polychrome decoration and lacquer. Xochimilco, Mexico, before 1982. L. 19 cm, 18.5 cm and 9.7 cm.

Besides folk toys, on the Indian sub-continent there are also 'ethnic' toys, the products of members of smaller ethnic groups or tribes, which sometimes compete with folk toys of neighbouring nations and nationalities. Confusingly, 'ethnic' toys do not always reflect the styles and tradition of the people who make them. They are sometimes copied from a neighbouring ethnic group.

In Bengal the biggest toymaking centre is probably Calcutta, particularly the Kumartali district of the city, where simple painted dolls, genre figures and some mechanical toys (for instance, acrobats) are made, along with the ubiquitous figures of deities. The Nutagram locality is famous primarily for its baby dolls, while Krishnagar produces highly realistic genre figures. Jointed dolls, shiny with lacquer, are also known from Bengal.

In the state of Orissa the towns of Kadobahal and Sambalpur specialized in animals on wheels, and in the city of Puri, figures were made relating to the cult of

Vishnu or Jagannath, whose famous temple is located in the city. The well-known figures of standing or sitting tigers, standing elephants and other animals, in various sizes and brightly painted colours (yellow and red predominating) also come from this region. The manner of painting these animals reveals a close affinity to the folk paintings which in recent decades have made Puri and Orissa state famous. Lacquered wooden rattles are also produced there. In Madhya Pradesh there is a production centre of lacquered objects, including toys, called Rewa. Benares in Uttar Pradesh is one of only a few toymaking centres which in the past were of national importance: according to historical reports, ox-drawn carts, dolls and dishes were traded to many other areas of the sub-continent.

Bombay, Pune and Nasik in Maharashtra supplied markets with brightly painted figures of domestic and wild animals, such as swans, cows, elephants, hens, tigers, rats, bears, dogs and pea-

113 Miniature guitar, wood with polychrome decoration. Mexico, before 1982. L. 39 cm, w. 11.6 cm.

cocks. Other 19th-century toys come from the territory of what was formerly the state of Savantvadi, renowned for its lacquered products. Lathe-turned toys, such as dishes, cups, rattles, etc., were assembled from several sections and painted in a simple geometric design with alternating stripes; several layers of lacquer were then added. The main source of the makers' income, however, was lacquered furniture, dishes and playing cards. Despite its great tradition, this whole craft industry practically vanished before the end of the 19th century.

Among outstanding toymaking centres whose products were carried to the whole world, predominantly by tourists, are certain towns in the state of Andhra Pradesh. Of these the most famous is Kondapalli, where carved scenes are produced based on everyday life. The toymakers show artisans at work, merchants displaying their goods, parades of elephants with local rulers and courtiers, and indigenous soldiers. These genre figures, sometimes grouped into little scenes and always painted in brilliant colours, can be re-

garded as toys as well as souvenirs. Figures of gods, various birds, animals and models of fruit and vegetables are also produced. In the towns of Tirupathi and Tiruchanur and their environs only carved, unpainted toys are made. These include figures of elephants and horses and horseback riders. Carvers work with sandalwood and make stylized animals and people, preferring to leave them in the natural colours of the wood. As in a number of other Indian toymaking centres, in these towns the main source of the woodcarvers' income is sacred objects and utilitarian items.

In Tamil Nadu state and its capital Madras figures on a stucco base are decorated with painting; many have found their way into European museums within the past century. From Jaipur in Rajasthan and its surrounding district come figures of the heroes of medieval epics in the form of figural toys or as marionettes, again brightly painted. The free-standing women's figures with raised arms perhaps originally represented a local goddess.

The painted, turned figures of Katha-

A

B

C

114 European ox-drawn wagons, all made of wood with polychrome decoration:
(A) Old Nuremberg type from the 19th century.
(B) Poultry cart from Berchtesgaden, where wagons drawn by three or four pairs of horses were also made, modern copy of a traditional toy.
(C) Wagon from north-eastern Poland, 20th century.
(D) Two carts from Yavorov, Lvov region, Ukraine, 1950s.

kali dancers from Kerala state are regarded as the best costumed dolls of the entire Indian subcontinent. They are made in the cities of Palghat, Trivandrum and Trichur, and in a number of localities on the Malabar coast.

In Burma the craftsmen in Rangoon carved wooden marionettes. In recent times they have used plywood, as well as traditional materials, as in the illustration of an animal-drawn cart. From Java in Indonesia come wooden figures of men and women with painted clothes. The bodies often have a basically triangular form, probably originating in a wooden stick split at one end.

Scrolls, prints and literature generally authenticate the existence of a toymaking craft in China at an early time. From the

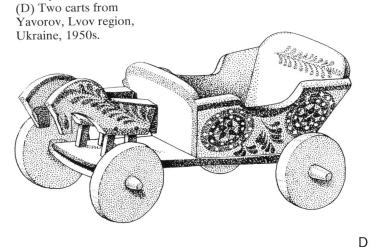

D

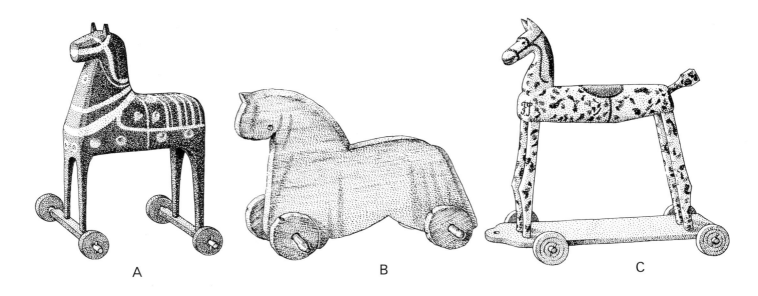

A   B   C

115 Horses on wheels,
(A) wood with polychrome
decoration. Vologda area,
Russia, 20th century.
H. 25 cm.
(B) wood, Egypt, Roman
period.
(C) wood with polychrome
decoration. Domažlice area,
Bohemia, 20th century.

9th century, vendors of toys regularly appear in stories and pictures, and the toys shown there are known throughout much of Asia. For instance, in a picture called 'One Hundred Children', from the 16th/17th century, are little boys on hobby-horses with drums and wooden rattles. Some toys almost certainly originated in China, such as the European *diabolo* or yo-yo, a toy in the form of a spool that falls and rises on a string. In China the yo-yo is shaped like an hour glass and the child keeps it bouncing on a tight string. When enough speed has been generated, the yo-yo can be released from the string

into the air and caught again by the string. (Or so it is said!) This wooden turned toy made its way to Europe probably in the late 18th century.

In Mongolia making wooden toys was a popular male pastime. In contrast to the older traditional toys, usually depicting various animals but looking very stiff and unnatural, today's toys are more dynamic, but perhaps less 'authentic'. They have a suggestion of the souvenir about them, and it is obvious that the carvers used chessmen as models for figures. In the more distant past wooden toys were a great rarity and Mongolian children

116 Chinese toy using the swinging of the weight under the board to move the tiger's jaws and the heads of the kneeling Chinese. Wood with polychrome decoration. Before 1957. L. 20 cm, h. 3.5 cm.

102

played with pebbles, from which they built simulated villages and herds of animals.

In 19th-century Siberia the Chuvash people made toy horse-drawn sledges and winged horses from scraps of wood. Though none has survived, they are known from more recent pieces.

From the European viewpoint, Japan is the most distant part of the Asian continent, but Japanese toymaking was certainly not a fringe activity. This is clear from a mere list of the basic types of wooden toys. In the Tokugawa period (1600—1868), preceding Japan's industrialization, the existence of at least 100 toymaking centres is reported.

Among the best-known types of Japanese toys, and at present among the most popular souvenirs for Europeans, is the turned, and usually painted, dolls in the shape of a skittle — the so-called *kokeshi.* There are several theories regarding its origin. According to one, the roots lie in the worship of the gods who protected the household. According to another, these dolls are phallic symbols connected with a fertility cult. A third theory draws a comparison with the development of Central European toymaking centres. The dolls were first produced in the Tohoku district of north-eastern Japan, where there were professional turners who moved from one place to another in search of suitable wood. Some time about the beginning of the 18th century they began to settle near hot springs. Bathing in these springs was widely popular and visitors often bought bowls and plates from the turners. These craftsmen, with an eye to the souvenir trade, then shifted from dishes to dolls. It would appear that the history of the *kokeshi* is only about 200 years old (poor support for the fertility-cult theory), and to this day in the Tohoku district similar human figures are made, as are painted and lacquered boxes. Folk *kokeshi* are produced in six northern prefectures (Miyagi, Yamagata, Iwate, Aomori, Akita and Fukushima), whose products can be divided into about ten basic types, though from the viewpoint of construction, they can be reduced to three. In the first the whole figure is made from a single piece of wood on the lathe. In the second, the body is produced separately, and the head and neck inserted into it. The head can usually turn and may incorporate a whistle. In the third type, the body and neck are made separately and the head is first inserted into the neck. It usually turns but does not whistle. Apart from a single type in white wood made in Manamaki in Iwate prefecture the other types of *kokeshi* are painted.

Among Japanese toys, probably the oldest are the carved figures of roosters, hens, eagles, rabbits and other animals which come from the Sasano district of Yamagata prefecture. According to oral tradition, they were made during the winter months and represented a secondary source of income for the local farmers. Not even here was toymaking an isolated process but stemmed from broader wood-carving traditions, which included, for example, the making of wooden flowers — sacrificial items for the local gods.

Some of today's toys are symbols of legends associated with a sanctuary or temple, or tell the story of a historical event. For example, painted horses from Miharu in Fukushima prefecture, originally made for the temple there, are linked with the legend of the sanctuary's founder, the military leader Sakanoue no Tamuramaro. Around the year A.D. 801, this general waged a war against eastern tribes, probably against the Ainu. During a decisive battle, 100 wooden votive horses in Kijomizu Dera temple came to life and hastened to help the Japanese army. In tribute to this victory, saddled horses are carved to this day. Visitors to the sanctuary buy them for their children's health and good physical growth. The horse is traditionally considered a sacred beast; it is also the seventh symbol of the Far Eastern zodiac and qualities such as nobility, energy and the ability to win public approval are popularly attributed to it. Other figures of the Zodiac — the rat, buffalo, tiger, rabbit, dragon, snake, lamb, monkey, rooster, dog and wild boar — are frequent subjects of folk toys, and adults give them to children as good-luck gifts.

A block of wood resembling the figure of a bullfinch, with feathers made of shavings, is associated with Dazaifu sanctuary on Kyü-shü Island. Figures of bullfinches, known as *uso,* are part of annual rituals conducted there.

Painted fish on wheels looking like large bream are made for the Fuji festival organized at Kokubu sanctuary on Kyü-shü Island. In the past they were used as

117 Movable toys using a simple mechanical principle:
(A) The monkey climbs down the ladder. Wood with polychrome decoration. China, before 1956. H. 51 cm.
(B) By squeezing or releasing, the crossed threads become tighter and turn the gymnast on his trapeze. Wood with polychrome decoration. Mexico, before 1982. H. 21.5 cm.
(C) The jumping tiger, lacquer on a wooden core. Olinalá, Mexico, before 1982. L. 32 cm.

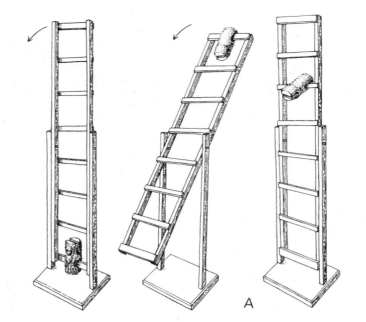

A

amulets against smallpox and their shape is, perhaps, derived from the legend about prazhma, one of a set of old Japanese Kodzhiki myths. Typical Kyü-shü figures are cock quails on wheels. Originally they were made in about thirty localities of Saga, Kumamoto, Fukuoka, Oita and Kagoshima prefectures, but today many of these workshops have disappeared. The quails come with two or four wheels and the live model is sometimes hard to discern in the toy. They apparently originated in the area around the Hisamine and Hokke-date temples, where they were used for cult purposes.

In many temples in the country, little hexagonal columns are sold as toys or as protective amulets. They probably came to Japan with Buddhism and their shape seems to be of phallic origin. Tradition links their first appearance with Kokubu temple. According to legend, the god Sasanoo once visited a rich man and asked him for a night's lodging. He was refused and found refuge in the house of the wealthy man's poor brother. As payment for his stay, the god gave his host such a device and advised him to place it on the gate during epidemics, saying it would protect the whole farmstead.

The wooden and brightly painted lion masks also have their roots in Buddhism. Besides masks, painted clappers in the form of a lion's head are found. The lion is regarded as an animal able to protect both the living and inanimate objects such as temples from evil spirits. Children in lion masks appear in many processions and dances.

Apart from those related to religious beliefs toys in Japan are drawn from daily life. Among them are model cottages on wheels, made in Tokushima prefecture. In the cottages is an indigo mill which is activated when the wheels turn. Similar mill-toys exist in other parts of the world such

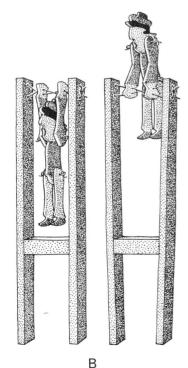

B

C

104

118   Rattle in the shape of
a tiger's head, wood with
polychrome decoration.
China, before 1965.
H. 22.5 cm, w. 5.6 cm.

119   Clapper in the shape of a drummer
with two drums, wood with polychrome
decoration. China, before 1956. Clappers
from China are found in the form of a bow
and arrow; as the arrow leaves the bowstring,
it makes a noise. H. 11.5 cm, l. 13 cm.

120   A tiger threatening two Chinese — mechanical toy, wood with
polychrome decoration. China, before 1957. Based on the same principle, and
made in China, are a flock of hens pecking grain or a camel or a horse swaying
in rhythm, with the pendulum acting as the head and the tail.
L. 20 cm, h. 3.5 cm.

121　Nest of Darumas, hollow figures that
fit into one another, wood with polychrome
decoration. Japan, before 1906. As Far
Eastern art became more popular, Japanese
toys were imported into Europe in the
second half of the 19th century.
H. 1.5—7.5 cm.

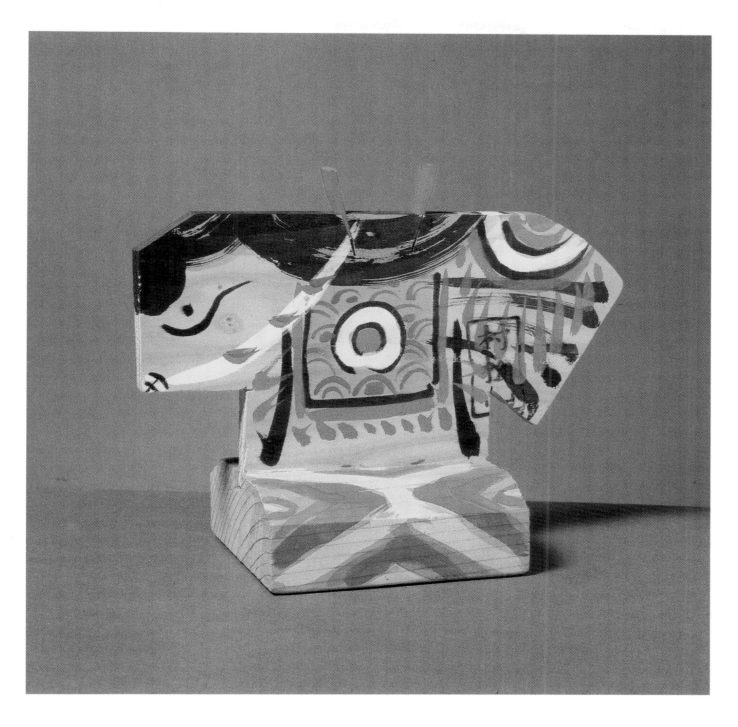

122 Horse of wooden board with
polychrome decoration. Muramatsu
sanctuary, Tokai village, Japan, before 1969.
This documents the ancient roots of the
so-called 'ema' votive gifts which go back to
the 8th century. The word 'ema' is written
with two Chinese characters meaning
'painted horse'. This gift was intended to
encourage the gods to favour the donor.
Besides a horse, there were figures of
petitioners as well. H. 15.5 cm, l. 19 cm.

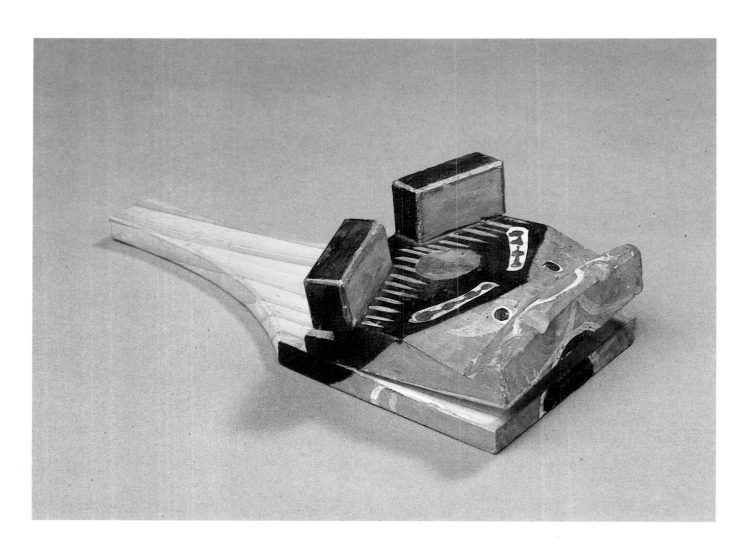

123　Clapper in the shape of a lion's head, wood with polychrome decoration. Japan, before 1925. L. 17.2 cm, w. 7.4 cm.

124   Quail on wheels, wood with
polychrome decoration. Setaka in Fukuoka
prefecture, Kyü-shü Island, Japan, before
1969. H. 6.5 cm, l. 17.5 cm.

125   Small chest with lid, wood with
polychrome decoration. Hitoyoshi in
Kumamoto prefecture, Kyü-shü Island,
Japan, before 1969. H. 5.5 cm, l. 9.2 cm,
w. 6.1 cm.

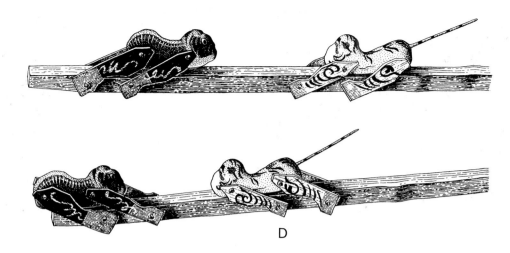

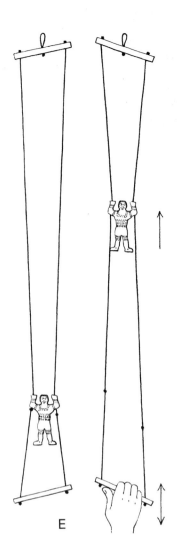

117 (D) A tiger chasing a monkey moves by tilting. Ceramic with wood and polychrome decoration. Mexico, before 1982. L. 124 cm, h. figure 13.5 cm. (E) A gymnast on strings, wood with polychrome decoration. Mexico, before 1982.

as Bohemia. In Japan in the last 100 years a number of new wooden folk toys have come into being — models such as trains and shops on wheels.

In North Africa, the tradition of toy-making goes back to prehistory. This is supported chiefly by finds of ancient Egyptian playthings, mentioned earlier. In sub-Saharan Africa we know about the development of wooden toy production only from the past two centuries, through the reports of travellers, colonial officials and soldiers. A second important source of information is the toys themselves. In all of black Africa wooden toys are always carved. An adze was used for preliminary work on the block of wood and a knife for the detailing. However, quite often the carver completed the whole job with an adze. At present, chisels are also used, having been introduced during the 19th century by missionaries and colonial officials. The finished figures are baked and rubbed with oil to give them a patina, and sometimes decorated with paint made of clay and organic dyes, or oil colours.

Dolls produced by professional African carvers are part toys and part sacred objects, frequently being used in initiation rites for adolescent girls. Wooden dolls correspond to individual ethnic, local and personal artistic styles and tend not to cross ethnic borders, although in some parts of Africa today toymaking centres export their products on a continental scale.

Among the most interesting African wooden toys are stylized human figures of several types. Many found their way to Europe, having been acquired by members of ethnographic expeditions in the

early years of the twentieth century. One particular type of female figure has a narrow conical body with a suggestion of breasts, but without hands; the head and face are usually shaped schematically. The doll is dressed in a short skirt, and was meant to ensure fertility — childless women carried them on their hips in the same way as children are carried. However, children also played with these dolls, presumably because they had served their purpose.

Stylized wooden dolls called *rad kamba* (child doll) are found among the Mossi people of Burkina Faso (formerly Upper Volta). Their simple and schematic resemblance to a woman's body indicates that their creators were as aware of children's fantasy when playing games as were the creators of Central European stylized wooden toys. In the same category are dolls from the Ashanti, Fanti and other West African coastal groups. They are generally known under the Ashanti name *akua-ba*. Whereas in silhouette a rounded head is typical of the Ashanti figures, the Fanti adopt an elongated, rectangular shape. They represent the model of beauty, a symbol of fertility and are both toys and amulets. Figures from the Goemai in central Nigeria and those of the Kanuri of Nigeria and Chad fall into the same category of stylized dolls.

Yoruba girls in present-day western Nigeria, play with flat dolls bearing symbols of Eshu, an intermediary between people and gods, on the bodies. Without his presence and assistance, petitions applying for supernatural powers will not be fulfilled: these Yoruba dolls are therefore amulets. They are found in more realistic form with

113

a profiled, carved head and small breasts, as well as in the purely stylized form of a rectangular block with a triangle on the neck serving as a head. They are usually decorated with burned stripes or painted with organic dyes.

The only large toymaking centre in West Africa is in eastern Nigeria, the land of the Ibo. Production is concentrated primarily in the localities of Ikot Ekpene, Ishan and surrounding districts. Besides stylized human, predominantly female figures, those of animals are likewise produced. Woodcarvers make figures of richly carved gods and figurally decorated masks. The toys are traditionally painted: in the past, colours were derived from organic materials, but today, for the most part, oil colours are used. As well as the dogs, lions, tigers, crocodiles, hens and roosters familiar in African markets and European museums, one finds figures of horseback riders, policemen, rowers and all kinds of spirits. Although they now have the character of toys, or cheap souvenirs, in the past such pieces were used for cult purposes. Many represented ancestors. Others were placed in sanctuaries and perhaps were both offerings as well as receivers of offerings. In the territory of the Ibibio and Ibo some dolls were made which were intended exclusively as toys. They are standing women's figures with fairly broad hips and short arms; the palms of the hands are raised to shoulder height facing the viewer. They come either in natural wood or are painted with a white clay, with simple decoration consisting of multi-coloured lines. Aside from individual figures, there are groups, for instance, of rowers in a dugout canoe. Their existence is authenticated from the end of the 19th century, when they were made in Ikot Ekpene and Ishan.

Among the few professionally made Central African toys are the phallus-like dolls from Kuba in Zaire. The elongated body continues to the head, shown in low relief, and male and female sex symbols are indicated on the doll. Dolls from the Wemba people of Zaire are also elongated but they differ from the Kuba version by having a removable head and fully fashioned facial features. Mention should also be made of the dolls of the Chokwe of Zaire and Angola, intended chiefly to ensure fertility in women.

The dolls of the Zaramo and other Swahili-speaking tribes, such as the Doe, Kami and Kerewe in Tanzania and Kenya, also have education, cult and play functions. They belong to the category of stylized figures with a conical body and distinguishable head and play an important role in initiation rites of girls. The girls, living apart from others, look after their dolls as they would real children, and they are taught not only how to handle little children but also about sexual life.

Male and female figures used in initiation rites and for children's games are familiar from a number of peoples living in the southern part of the African continent — from the Venda, Gwamba, Lozi, Chopi, Ndebele and Zulu, among others. These are more realistic, having hands and legs as well as distinguishable facial features. The design corresponds to the style of local carvers in decorating human figures in general.

We have concentrated on dolls which are specialities of professional toymakers. Figures of animals also appear sporadically. Among the Luba of Zaire and Zambia the elephant often features, the body decorated by painting and burning. The figure of the elephant from the Ngwato of Botswana is decorated in a similar manner.

Traditional American Indian cultures are rich in professionally made ceramic toys, but wooden toys by professionals are less common. They are found mainly among craftsmen coming from or working for people of European background, or among mixed populations who have adopted European models and values. The American continents are territories where three different cultural traditions mingle: Amerindian, African and European. In the 19th and 20th centuries, Indian professionals made wooden toys mainly by traditional carving, using knives and chisels; craftsmen working for whites or mixed-race customers used the lathe also.

The Seminole Indians first began carving toys in the 20th century under the influence of missionaries. Prior to their attempt to find an outlet for the sale of toys as a regular business, production of wooden girl dolls predominated; in contrast wooden boy dolls were a great rarity. But because the figures sold better in pairs, production was extended to boy dolls as well. At first the figures were without hands and only at the insistence of the

126 Parrot on a stand, wood with polychrome decoration. Bohemia, before 1945. Thematically it probably draws on circus scenes and exotic regions. H. 14 cm, w. 9 cm.

missionaries did the carvers begin to add arms, often movable. Again on the recommendation of the missionaries a new type of toy was introduced — the horseback rider. The figures are either painted by the carvers or given a painted head, the body being dressed in clothes.

In the south-western United States one comes across a very old tradition of wooden figures representing spirits. They are known as *kachina*, a term used both for the spirits and the dancers who embody the spirits during religious ceremonies. The oldest find of a *kachina* is from a grave attributed to the Casas Grandes culture, about 1300—1426. The oldest examples of modern *kachinas* come from the end of the 19th century; in the 20th century and particularly following the Second World War, their production was expanded and today they are among the most popular items sold in Indian souvenir shops. The large number of spirits naturally differs in appearance considerably, and the ingenuity of Hopi and Pueblo carvers is devoted to producing figurines of many shapes and sizes. The Pueblo and Hopi children linked wooden *kachina* figurines not only with the idea of a gift but also with the discovery of their living personification — masked dancers representing the different spirits.

Wooden toys also appeared in the most northern regions of North America. Eskimo girls not only played with dolls carved from walrus tusks but also owned wooden dolls, while boys had wooden boats. To amuse Indian children living in British Columbia and Alaska, miniature wooden masks were carved, similar to those used by adults, and wooden ship models are also known.

The toys of many American settlers in the 19th and early 20th centuries did not go beyond the repertoire of folk toys made at the time in Europe, such as horseback riders, with a great variety of animals, figures of acrobats and movable toys such as pecking hens. In view of the fact that from the 16th and more particularly the 17th century European toys, especially Central European, were exported to the North American continent, this connection is no surprise. Among the U.S. toymaking centres were Springfield, Massachusetts, and various towns of Pennsylvania. Other workshops existed in Ohio. Typically, Pennsylvanian 19th-century production follows the Dutch and German folk tradition. Foretelling the end of folk toymaking were figures and silhouettes of people and animals covered with printed paper. They sometimes formed part of genre scenes such as circus menageries, and were produced in workshops in Rhode Island and parts of Massachusetts.

A considerable amount of information about toymaking workshops comes from Mexico, where woodcarving and the use of lacquer were established before the Europeans arrived: archaeological finds in Yucatan have shown that the Mayas used lacquer. In the decades after the conquest of Mexico by the Spaniards, the level of most traditional crafts declined, but during the later colonial period they were gradually revived.

At the present time an important centre for making wooden toys is the state of Guanajuato, an area famous for its mining traditions in the colonial period. Not only wooden toys are produced, but also playthings of papier mâché, metal, and straw (a material duscussed below). Besides the capital city Guanajuato, the centres are principally the towns of Santa Cruz de Juventino Ross, Celaya and Irapuato. The carvers first use machetes for the rough shaping, then carve the details with knives. The figures are always coloured. Painted figures of boxers, tightrope walkers, painted boxes and figures of death are produced here, especially before All Souls' Day. Painted miniature furniture and market stalls are also made.

In the state of Michoacán, the centre of the production of toys is the town of Zirahuán, but much better known are the towns of Pátzcuaro and Uruapán, where lacquered objects are produced. The toys are painted in rich colours and decorated with the motif of flowers on a light or dark base. The toymakers are inspired by scenes from everyday life and by religious beliefs, but they also make carousels, Russian wheels and *voladores* — figures of participants in traditional rituals which hang by their arms on a carousel and fly through the air. Lacquered items, drawing on the same subject-matter, are also made in Olinalá in Guerrero state.

Another important centre is the capital, Mexico City, and nearby towns like San Antonio de la Isla.

Besides the above-mentioned toys,

Mexico also produces toys associated with Christian holidays, for example, Easter rattles. In the last few decades a number of woodcarvers have begun to use modern materials such as plywood, making Russian wheels or rod puppets in this material. Miniature musical instruments — fiddles, guitars, mandolins, trumpets and all sorts of rattles — are also made there.

The earliest-known Argentinian toys are no older than the 20th century. Besides furniture, building sets and drums, many toys on wheels were produced — animals, carts and carriages. Well-known workshops were concentrated in the suburbs of Buenos Aires.

There were some toymaking workshops in Brazil, the production centres being the capital Rio de Janeiro, and Santos, together with smaller adjacent communities.

Wooden toys of the indigenous inhabitants of Oceania and Australia were mainly fashioned at home and there seem to have been no professional toymakers. European colonists who settled in Australia and the Pacific islands imported toys and it is likely that local products were made in imitation, but few are documented.

It would be difficult even to estimate the extent of trade in wooden toys because the only documentary evidence comes from Europe. Yet the European trade was on a world scale. Wooden toys from Nuremberg were exported in the 16th and 17th centuries to Latin America, the Caribbean Islands and India. Eighteenth-century accounts indicate that toys circulated throughout the entire European continent. House-to-house pedlars and merchants who travelled across the whole of Europe and set up warehouses were responsible for such sales. For example, in the 18th and 19th centuries, objects from the Tirol were sold in Germany, the Austrian Empire, as well as in Italy, France, the Netherlands, Portugal and Russia.

If we have come across the same type of toys in widely different places, it is certainly not by chance, because dolls, soldiers, carts and animals correspond best to the needs of children at play in practically every culture. Furthermore, the principles of mechanical wooden toys are repeated in different countries because those principles represent the limit of practical possibilities in peasant societies.

Snakes that squirm from side to side are familiar in India, China and Japan, as well as Central Europe. They differ only in material and decoration: in the Far East they are made of bamboo canes, in Mexico and Europe of wood. The pecking hen is known in Central Europe and in India; the principle of the pendulum which sets the limbs of figures in motion can be found in laundresses washing at the tub in England, a horse with a nodding head in Russia, or a tiger baring its teeth menacingly at two kneeling persons in China. Toys activated by two sticks pulling in opposite directions, the principle of the Russian toy of the smith and the bear, are familiar in Central Europe, the United States, Mexico and Egypt. Mechanical toys based on the scissors principle are common throughout Europe, as is the jointed monkey or squirrel (sometimes a sailor) climbing a pole.

In the second half of the 19th century, the simple toys that moved down or up an inclined plane became widespread in Europe. The principle of these 'walking' dolls and animals was employed in numerous very popular devices. Around the mid-19th century toys propelled by rotating circular bases began to be made, and also dancing couples on a circular base that was set in motion by pulling a string. Engravings from Savoy and Naples prove that street musicians used them to attract attention from passers-by.

The historical roots of many of these mechanical principles must be sought in the Far East, especially in China. The principle of movable figures, operated by turning the wheels of an animal-drawn carriage, was known there from about the 2nd century B.C. Reports of magnetic toys date from the lst millennium A.D. and toys using the principle of bamboo springs (for instance, figures opening doors and windows, movable musicians) were known in China for several centuries before they were first adopted in Europe. In the past, the knowledge of mechanical toys or principles spread slowly. Today, when the possibilities of mutual inspiration among folk artists are far greater, we still find locally contrived mechanical principles in the more remote parts of the world, while, at the same time, simple mechanical, factory-made toys may often be an inspiration to unsophisticated producers.

117

Professional Toymakers: Ceramics

Because the material is not subject to rot and decay, ceramic toys are the oldest, reasonably authentic, survivals. Certain objects which archaeologists have discovered in Neolithic sites are generally believed to have served as toys, on the basis of an analogy with much later times, certain proof being impossible. These prehistoric ceramic playthings, which come from the New World as well as the Old, were of course made by 'amateurs'. However, because of the technical processes involved, most ceramic toys are the work of professional makers.

In pre-industrial times, toys were seldom the main output of a particular craftsman or workshop, although there were cases of wooden toys fulfilling that function. Potters, it can safely be said, never produced toys as their main product. In European workshops at least, toys in pottery were always a secondary preoccupation, made by apprentices learning the trade, or by journeymen and masters when they had no more important work on hand. This was true also, for example, in Bengal. There, potters were chiefly occupied in making statues of gods for religious celebrations, but at slack periods they turned out playthings too. Among the Hausa and the Ibo in Nigeria, potters modelled miniature items to sell at the market, and these may have been similar in purpose to the small dishes made in Europe as a form of advertising, which were sometimes given to the children of customers as a little bonus on the sale.

Dishes were usually modelled on a wheel while figures of various kinds were shaped by hand. Some draw a distinction between the production of dishes, a craft activity, and the making of figures, which allows greater scope for personal taste and artistic expression. Modelled clay toys were fired and painted, sometimes before glazing, sometimes after (if glazed at all). Toys made of dried clay, or plaster, or other similar preparations, form a special group.

In comparing miniature pieces, or toys, with the normal output of a particular pottery, it is not surprising to find that the one type resembles the other. However, potters seem to have often reverted to their own salad days when making toys, since older types and patterns, discarded for general business, often crop up.

Not only the forms of miniature ceramic dishes were drawn from the dishes (and other ware) produced for the adult market, the decoration too was directly related to decoration of adult ceramics, depending on the technical capacity of the potters' workshops. Only undecorated ware was produced in Europe in the 13th and 14th centuries, so far as we know, but during the 15th century coloured glazes became more common, reflecting the increasing quantity of glazed ware generally. This relationship is confirmed by research and contemporary reports of the practices of potters. For example, the Moravian and Slovak workshops of the Habaners (Anabaptists), members of a Protestant sect from Germany and Switzerland, greatly influenced the local folk culture in the 16th and 17th centuries thanks to their superior quality. They supplied markets with sets of miniature coloured dishes, whose decoration was identical with their full-size plates, bowls and pitchers. Another example is the Chilean pottery centre of Quinchamalí, where miniature dishes were made with incised decoration filled with white paste, similar to the general output.

In contrast to toys of other materials, ceramic toys appear only in certain localities. Trade in ceramic toys reached large areas, but it never attained the scope or extent of the trade in wooden toys, even though it was organized from large commercial centres such as Nuremberg. Although ceramic toys travelled, it was primarily on a countrywide or statewide basis, and only during the 19th century did this pattern change. In Europe before the 19th century, strict guild regulations and local protectionist policies stemming from them prevented wider circulation of potters' products. Only when the guild system was abolished did goods begin to be exported. Potters produced items for sale to middlemen, for instance, travelling circuses or gypsies, whose wagons transported them far and wide. Smaller shipments were circulated by pedlars. In this way, the products of one workshop might spread over hundreds of kilometres. Reports have survived of the smuggling of ceramic toys. For instance, the pearl workers of Bohemia, who were employed in Bavaria, brought figures from Bavarian potteries to the Czech side of the border. The individual figures were commonly for Nativity scenes, though they were also used as toys.

Among the most common ceramic toys were dolls, standing figures with their legs joined (or without legs, but a bell-shaped skirt concealing their absence). Sometimes these are individual female figures; sometimes they hold a child in their arms or on their backs. They are usually not very tall, often no more than 15 cm high. They were a favourite item of Russian potters, coming from all the main Russian ceramic areas of the 19th and 20th centuries, such as Orlov, Ryazan, Tambov, Kursk, Voronezh, Tula and Kaluzh. The motif of the woman or mother carrying a child is also found in Indonesia, Borneo, Thailand, Peru, Bolivia and elsewhere.

Ceramic dolls dating back to ancient times are known from archaeological excavations in the Near East, although discussion continues as to whether these objects, found in tombs, were gifts, miniatures substituting for articles intended for use, or toys. Some ceramic figures of women are widely agreed to be dolls, for example, 3rd-millennium B.C. figures from the Mohenjo-Daro and Harappa culture in the Indus valley. What are certainly dolls are known from Greek and Roman times. During the festival of Sat-

127 Money-box, jug and double-cup, glazed ceramic. Koloveč, Bohemia, before 1913. The dishes are replicas of those used by adults. H. money-box 7.5 cm, jug 8.2 cm, double-cup 6.7 cm.

128 Miniature dishes and animals, smoked and polished ceramic. From the pottery centre in Quinchamalí, Chile, before 1938. H. 2.3—8.5 cm.

urnalia in Rome, they were distributed to both adults and children. Similar figures were known in medieval Europe: some were made in Nuremberg and some in Prague about the end of the 14th century. Otherwise, most finds of female figures date from no earlier than the 15th century. Such figures are common enough more or less everywhere during the past two centuries, however.

In the Ancient World, a popular toy was a miniature horse, or horse and rider. The appearance of this ceramic figure goes back to pre-Christian times, when the horse was regarded as a symbol of youth, of vital force and natural renewal. Ceramic figures of riders are authenticated from Egypt from about 500 B.C. They were also made in medieval Europe and it is assumed that they depict knights. This motif is also frequently found in combination with a whistle, as in examples from Querfurt, Thuringia, Čáslav in Bohemia, Prague, and other towns. More recently,

similar finds have been made in such towns as Strasbourg and Nuremberg.

Other favourite ceramic toys were figures of animals. They vary according to the individual workshop but in terms of quantity they cannot compete with dolls or horses.

Miniature dishes were found in a grave of the (Iron Age) Hallstatt period at Muschenheim, Germany, and other sets from Bohemia have been dated to the 5th century B.C. Models of boats on wheels were made in Mesopotamia in the 2nd millennium B.C. Wagons are known also from the Mohenjo-Daro culture. Probably some early ceramic discs, usually described as wheels, were a kind of ancient top.

The whistle unquestionably holds first place among ceramic toys. It is found throughout the world in all sorts of forms — as figures of people, animals or various utility objects. Whistles also take the shape of musical instruments: recorders,

129   Doll with infant on
her back, ceramic and fabric.
Guatemala, 1970s.
H. 11.5 cm.

ocarinas or little fiddles. Sometimes forms overlap; for instance, Croatian whistles have a bird's body but the heads are those of horses or cattle and some of them carry a rider.

As in the Old World, in America also the use of ceramic whistles goes back deep into the past. Figures of birds come from the territory of Panama and Colombia (the Chiriquí culture, c. A.D. 1000). From Ecuador (the Esmeralda culture, A.D. 1000—1500) come the well-known human figures, sometimes wearing clothes made of feathers, from Brazil (the Santarém culture, A.D. 1250—1500) come whistles shaped like armadillos or other animals. If we take into account whistles made of wood, bone, metal and other materials, then they are among the most widespread toys in the world.

European ceramic whistles were researched by Heide Nixdorf (see the Catalogue of the Berlin Ethnographic Museum). She divided them into three basic types: pot-shaped whistles, cylinder-shaped whistles, and water whistles, whose warbling tone is achieved by adding water to the body of the whistle. These three types are further broken down into twelve subgroups classified by overall structure. All three types are known from European countries; they are variously named 'cuckoo', 'nightingale', 'dove', 'canary', 'bird's whistle', or 'little jug'; in

130 Small items from Galicia, Ukraine (basket), and from Russia (jug), glazed ceramic. End of 19th century. H. jug 9.5 cm, basket 9.5 cm.

131 Set of birds, unglazed ceramic. Tunja village, Colombia, 1930s. H. 3—3.5 cm.

northern countries names include 'rooster' and 'trilling chick'. These, of course, are 19th- or 20th-century names; the oldest come from 13th-century France and are simpler: 'whistle' and 'bird's whistle'. The linking of the whistle with the figure of a bird or with a bird's name is universal. Bird forms are known from pre-

Columbian America, as well as ancient India, China and Japan.

Ceramic whistles are the exception to the rule of the small-scale export of ceramic toys. In the Middle Ages they were exported from the Rhineland and southern Germany to Northern Europe and it would seem that later folk pottery production there drew on these models. In similar fashion, Portuguese figures with a whistle in the base are known from French models, as local production only began in the 19th century. A popular type of water whistle was introduced by the Moravian Brethren (Protestant exiles) to the United States as early as the 18th century.

Whistles spread to the Arab world from Europe during the Crusades. The Arab historian, Ibn Rushd (Averroës) condemned them as a Christian toy and proposed that they be banned. In the 19th century rider-whistles were made, for example, in Egypt. Of course, in most parts of Asia whistles were known and used regardless of contacts with Europe.

Other musical ceramic toys popular throughout the world are rattles and bells. These usually take the form of balls, animals or fruits. Sometimes objects intended for adults had a rattle in the hollow

132 Ceramic doll from Nuremberg, 15th century.

133 Two views of a ceramic warrior figure. Silesia, second half of 14th century. In addition to dolls and riders, figures have also been found of mythical creatures, reflecting the thinking of the time on unknown creatures.

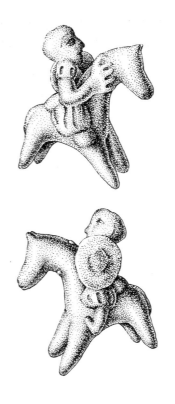

handle or legs or as applied ornament. Next to whistles, rattles are considered the oldest type of toy besides being probably the first with which a human being comes into contact. In Bohemia they were known in the 2nd millennium B.C., and in other parts of Central Europe they have been found in graves of the older Hallstatt period. One Roman rattle, in the form of a hen, was discovered in Worms, Germany.

In view of the fact that ceramic toys of baked clay and of different compositions such as plaster or mixtures of clay and glue, etc. were produced by the overwhelming majority of potteries throughout the world, it is impossible even to list them. We shall therefore focus on several ceramic or clay-type toys characteristic of a certain area or country.

A ceramic money-box is a typical European toy, often taking the form of a pig or cockerel. Reports from around 1900 mention money-boxes shaped as apples and lemons from Hesse, as dolls, human and animal figures from Bohemia, and as beehives. The beehive money-box is among the oldest types, having been found in Pompeii and Roman Britain. Examples of these have survived also from the Middle Ages in England, but we do not know whether they served as toys. The first authenticated ceramic money-box toys appeared in the 16th and 17th centuries — 'piggy banks' and beehives being common shapes. Within the past 200 years they were widespread in Italy, the Netherlands, Germany, Silesia, Bohemia and the Baltic region.

The spread of money-boxes became possible only at a time of relative economic stabilization, especially among the rural population. It can be assumed that originally they were the toys of urban children. Their popularity in the 19th century meant that folk potters vied with professional potteries to produce them, flooding city and country markets. Porcelain or earthenware money-boxes then took the form of swans, pears, monkeys, elephants, cockerels and pigs.

134 Boat on wheels, fired clay. From a child's grave, Warka locality, Iraq, 7th century B.C.

135 Bird whistles, polished and fired ceramic. Central Mexico, before 1900. The tradition of Central American and Mexican bird whistles dates from A.D. 1000. H. 6.3 cm and 5.4 cm.

Probably under European influence, the production of ceramic money-boxes was introduced to other continents, being found in Mexico in the form of a heart, symbolizing religious preoccupations. Their surface is richly ornamented with coloured glazes and decoration in relief. In contrast to this, the round, slightly flattened money-boxes from Yoruba workshops in Nigeria are decorated with simple slip painting.

A European speciality is the movable ceramic toy, or toys containing springs. These are figures of animals, birds, people and angels, attached to a base by a spring or coiled wire, which nod with every movement. They come from Cappel near Marburg in Hesse, Sonneberg in Thuringia and the Hlinsko district of Bohemia, among other places. The same principle appears in tin figures. The only overseas analogies are the Mexican figures of death, produced for All Souls', in which the body and limbs are joined by coiled wires.

One can trace the development of the production of toys as souvenirs by the spread of several types of ceramic playthings, in particular folk figures. This combination of the toy-souvenir has become especially common in modern times. From the end of the 18th century, European potters began to model toy figures in the form of typical local types: musicians in folk costume, Jewish pedlars, wood cutters, and peasants doing varied jobs. Figures appeared of American Indians, or based on a religious theme such as the Adam and Eve figures made at Lauterbach in Hesse. Painted and glazed figures were made for children as utilitarian objects, such as inkpots in the form of bears, horses, kitchen stoves or human figures from Hesse workshops, and it is hard to decide whether such products should be classed as toys.

125

137 European figural whistles, ceramic, slip-painting or glaze.
(A) Skorping locality, Jutland, Denmark, early 20th century.
(B) Lorca locality, Murcia, Spain, 1972.
(C) Colmar, Alsace, France, 1906.
(D) Agram locality, Croatia, early 20th century.

The development from the toy to the decorative art object is not confined to Europe alone, although it can best be traced using European materials. From the second half of the 19th century toys were produced in the form of genre scenes, such as the stalls of pottery sellers, Spanish bullfights or craftsmen practising their trade. In the 20th century this devel-opment has taken place with toys made in certain Asian workshops. For example, Dagestan folk potters working in the vil-lage of Balkhar (in the Caucasus, Russia), where pottery has been produced for several centuries, have diverted within the past thirty years to genre-scene toys which can hardly be said to be real toys. They encompass houses full of people and

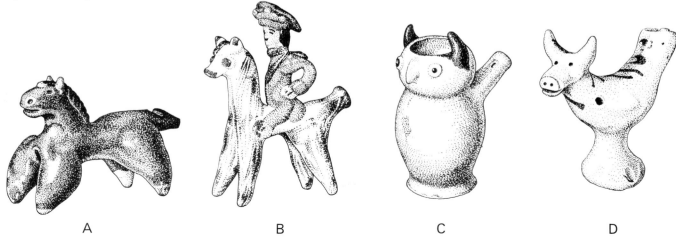

A   B   C   D

138 Seller of Spanish vases, glazed ceramic. Spain, before 1894. Example of a genre toy close to being a souvenir. H. 9.5 cm.

◄
136 Turkey-cock and goose in skirts, ceramic with painting on a plaster base. Dymkovo village (today Kirov), Russia, before 1945. Maker: J. Z. Koshkina. The dress and decoration of the animals probably comes from illustrations to stories or from fairy-tale texts. Dymkovo is one of the most outstanding pottery centres in Russia. The first references to toys being made there are from 1811. H. turkey-cock 17 cm, goose 15 cm.

(E) Barcelos locality, Portugal, mid-20th century.
(F) Dymkovo (today Kirov), Russia, 1971.
(G) Rumania, 1976.
(H) Stara Sil village, Sambir district, Ukraine, early 20th century.

E   F   G   H

139 Horseback rider, ceramic with slip painting. China, before 1965. Stylized compact group in which only the rider's head is visible. H. 7.3 cm, l. 7.5 cm.

140 Human figures and a horse, painted and lacquered ceramic. Bought at a market in Medinipur from a member of the Shankhakar caste, Egra village, Bengal, India, 1976. In addition to fired figures, dried clay, painted and, in some instances, lacquered examples — often representing animals — are found. H. figures 8.5 cm, and 10 cm, horses 9.8 cm, l. 10 cm.

128

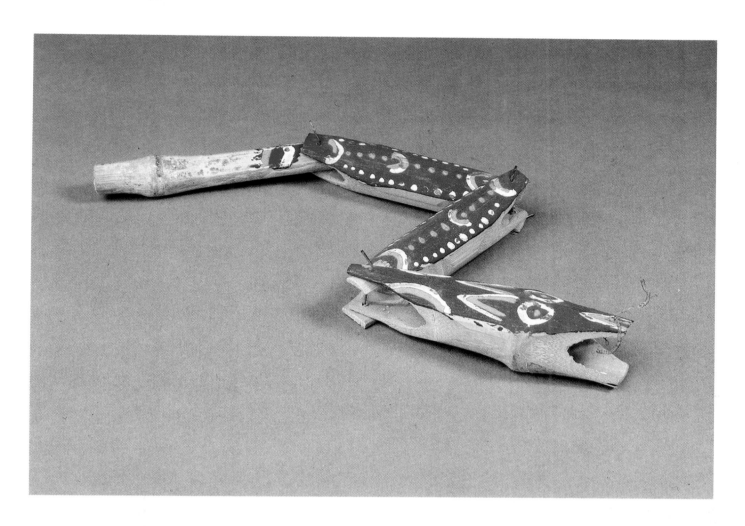

141   Movable snake. Japan, before 1925.
The body of the snake comprises several
jointed bamboo pieces with polychrome
decoration. Movable toys (snake, fish) are
made in the same way in India, Russia,
Rumania and other countries. In Bohemia
and Germany the joints of the snake's body
are halved and glued to a central tape.
L. 27.5 cm.

142   Animals from Ibo and Ibibio, wood
with polychrome decoration. Nigeria,
workshops of the 1960s. Today these are
both toys and souvenirs. H. elephant
16.5 cm, dog 24.5 cm, parrot 17 cm.

143 Doll with movable
arms, wood with polychrome
decoration. Ibibio, Nigeria,
before 1968. The same
figures can be seen in
sanctuaries or on cult mask
rods. H. 28.5 cm.

144 Doll on circular base, glazed ceramic. Stupava, Slovakia, before 1945. A utility item also used as a toy. The doll has no legs and stands on a wide, bell-shaped skirt. H. 24.5 cm, d. 9 cm.

145 Set of dishes, glazed ceramic.
Quezaltenango, Guatemala, before 1914.
Sets of several dozen pieces were shipped
in boxes filled with shavings. H. 7—10.5 cm.

146   Money-boxes, glazed ceramic.
Quezaltenango, Guatemala, before 1914.
One is in the shape of a Sacred Heart, the
other in the form of a hot chilli (pepper) with
the inscription 'Amistad' (Friendship).
H. pepper 22.5 cm, heart 19 cm.

147   Doll representing a half-caste woman,
glazed ceramic. Cochabamba, Bolivia, before
1964. This is a popular motif in Bolivia
and has existed since the 19th century.
H. 13.5 cm, d. 8.2 cm.

148   Old man with pipe and Jewish pedlar
carrying a bag on his back, glazed ceramic.
Domažlice, Bohemia, before 1945. The
clothing of the figures is similar to men's folk
costumes of the Domažlice district.
H. 15.2 cm and 14.5 cm.

149 Animal figures, only occasionally produced earlier by potters as toys, have become souvenir items in recent decades. The tortoise is from the Shipibo tribe of Venezuela, before 1985. L. 10.5 cm.

150 Ceramic figures of sitting bears made by potters living along the Rio Grande valley, New Mexico, U.S.A., in the Santa Clara Pueblo. They were acquired at the beginning of the 1930s. W. 5 cm and 3.5 cm, h. *c.* 7.5 cm.

151 Ceramic rattles in the form of a bird and a kitten. China, before 1956.

152 Genre figures of musicians — one with a pipe and the other a drum, of painted ceramic, with fabric whiskers, from one of the national minorities of China, before 1965. H. *c.* 5.5 cm.

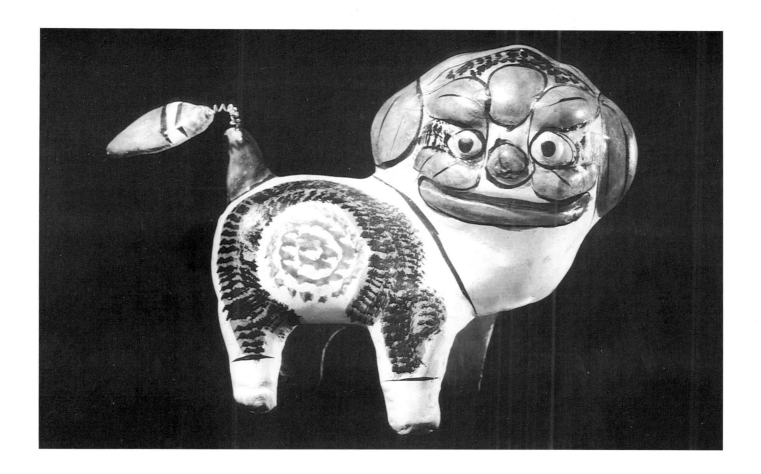

153 Lion, painted ceramic.
China, before 1965.
H. 10.3 cm, l. 13 cm.

stabled cattle, groups of farmers doing field work, and, appropriately, potters modelling bowls on a potter's wheel. Similarly, the workshops of American Indians of the south-western United States, apart from older types such as figures of animals and birds have, in the past 50 years, made models of pueblos, while terraced houses were made by the Hopi, Zuñi and Pueblo Indians.

The beginning of mass production of ceramic dolls in the state of Nevada in the U.S.A., in which potters of the Mohave, Yuma, Maricopa and Cocopa Indian tribes took part, also reflects the demand for souvenirs. Today these miniatures — painted and clothed — are part of the traditional art of Indians of the Colorado River basin. Aside from standing dolls, there are mothers with children in their arms and dolls in papooses. The decoration of faces and bodies represents the traditional face-painting and tattooing of women and men. Mass production began in the second half of the 19th century; the earlier examples were presumably used for cult purposes.

Ceramic toys drawing on local or na-

tional cultural or religious traditions in Asia were different from the customary animals, dolls and riders. In Bengal they typically resemble favourite gods — Kartik, the god of war, the gods Rama, Sita, Lakshman, Vishnu and his siblings, which are also made in wood.

In China, ceramic figural whistles showing the legendary monk Tripitaka on his journey to India with his animal guides, principally the monkey Sun Wu-k'ung, belong in this category. A journey full of adventures and encounters with all sorts of heroes, it has been often described in literature and drama.

Among other favourite subjects interpreted by Chinese potters and modellers were the animals of the Far Eastern zodiac, models for urban and rural architecture, and countless miniature portraits showing a great variety of types of China's inhabitants. Terracotta figures are known as well as stoneware and porcelain. In China, schools of specialists devoted themselves to modelling the varied genre figures, whose faithful depictions and overall artistic workmanship made them very desirable to collectors.

139

154 Whistles in the form
of a dog, ram and mounted
rider, painted and glazed
ceramic. Dog and rider come
from the Ukraine, before
1914; the ram is from Russia,
before 1889. H. dog 8.5 cm,
rider 9 cm, ram 7 cm.

155 Model of a hut,
ceramic with slip-painting.
Uvongo village, Zululand,
South Africa, 1970s. It is
similar to cult miniatures of
sacred huts of the traditional
rulers of South African
tribes, although, today, they
are souvenirs.
H. 9.5 cm, d. 7.5 cm.

A special feature are Chinese miniature ceramic rod puppets for children's theatres. They copy precisely the costumes of real actors.

From all over China, also, come ceramic toys that produce a sound, such as buzzers in the form of birds and cicadas hanging by threads at the end of poles which, when spun, buzz beautifully. Whistling and hooting toys also come in the form of birds and animal heads, using the principle of the bellows and the whistle.

In Japan ceramic toys with an educational intent are found, such as the famous group of three monkeys, one covering his eyes, the second his mouth and the third his ears. They express the advice 'see no evil, hear no evil and speak no evil', and are associated particularly with Kyü-shü Island in Kumamoto prefecture. Similar figures of children holding half a loaf of bread in their hands, produced in the city Kyoto, are intended to remind us of the inseparability of paternal and maternal love. Their creation is linked to the story of the clever child who, when asked whether he loved his father or mother more, broke the bread in two and inquired which half was the tastier.

Some Japanese ceramic toys are linked to temples, and originally served as votive gifts, though today they are bought predominantly as toys. Among them are the figures of boxes sold in temples in central Tokyo. In Tokyo and Osaka, figures of kittens waving one paw were produced and given to children for good luck. Ceramic figures of dogs are gifts for newborn boys and are supposed to protect them from evil. Around Nagasaki, genre figures of foreigners, normally European, in the dress of the 16th or 17th century, were made. Workshops in Kyoto produced figures of actors in costume.

In the area extending from Central Asia and the Caucasus to south-eastern and Eastern Europe, ceramics dominate the total output of professional toymakers. Among ceramic toys the commonest are whistles in the form of birds, horses, sheep, riders and dolls. Whether plain figures or whistles, they are glazed, sometimes partially, and sometimes painted over or under the glaze.

African ceramic toymaking is known only minimally. Besides whistles from various countries of North Africa, there are Ethiopian miniature animals and dishes with a fire-blackened surface which in recent decades have been sold both as toys and souvenirs. This black ware is made by the Falasha and Amhari-

156 Mounted rider and horses, glazed and unglazed ceramic. Cochabamba, Bolivia, 1964. Figures of riders and horses were unknown in pre-Columbian America. This type of toy was brought by Europeans, which explains its similarity to the European figures. H. 7.2—10.2 cm.

157 The first, and for many decades the only, find of ancient ceramic toys on wheels was made near Tres Zapotes, Mexico, in 1888. Only after 1940 were others found. Since then more than 20 such figures have been discovered, of jaguars, dogs, red deer and caymans. Made roughly from A.D. 800 until the Spanish conquest of Mexico in the 16th century. These are from Huamantla, Tlaxcala, Mexico, 800-1250.

potters, the latter having copied the method from their neighbours. The Zulu of southern Africa make traditional huts in miniature form, which nowadays must be regarded as souvenirs.

Pre-Columbian toys from Veracruz, Mexico, include dogs, jaguars and caymans on wheels. Dozens of wheeled figures have been discovered in graves, an interesting find since for a long time it was widely believed that ancient Mexicans did not know the wheel until it was introduced by Europeans. The 'toys' found in graves, which date from the early centuries A.D., prove that the wheel was known, but apparently only appreciated as a device for imparting mobility to toys.

We have insufficient information to answer questions about the size of past production of ceramic toys, or the range of objects included. Even for Europe, one must speculate. It would seem that a break occurred in the rising European production in the 16th century, but was the potters' production really increasing or is the greater number of finds due to the decreasing period of time between manufacture by the potters and discovery by the archaeologists? For the present, however, we can say on the basis of individual discoveries and local research that in the Middle Ages the range of ceramic toys was substantial, and that the types of objects made then were similar to those that were current in the 18th and 19th centuries.

Confectionery

Children were and are often given toys on certain days of the year — on major religious festivals, feast days or national holidays, and perhaps during more private celebrations within the family. This custom, which includes toys in general, is especially associated with gifts of sweets or candy and other things to eat. We may call such things 'edible toys'.

'Edible toys' appear mainly in countries where Christianity was established. Although similar customs no doubt occurred in non-Christian regions, we have little information concerning them, and here the emphasis will be on Europe and on countries where Christianity became established as a result of missionary activity and colonization.

The traditional food 'toy' was modelled from dough, by hand or with a mould, and was either sweet or savoury. Though edible, it was not necessarily intended to be eaten. In addition, similar confections were from various types of fruit (mentioned above), such as dried plums, figs, apples, pears, raisins and nuts.

Edible toys were made by professional craftsmen, such as bakers, gingerbread-makers and confectioners, and by ordinary people. Professional craftsmen sometimes prepared edible toys for members of disparate cultural groups. For example, in Galicia at the end of the 19th century, Ukrainian, Hutsul and Jewish cultural traditions mingled. All three prepared for their own holidays by taking their own edible toys, but the Jews also prepared and baked pastries in the form of horses and human figures for the Christian Ukrainians. The production centre of these pastries was the village of Kozová.

Festivities and holidays dictated the special shape of edible toys, which was based on local traditions or on generally accepted symbols. Obvious examples include the figure of St Nicholas and the devils associated with December celebrations of this Saint's day, or the sweets and chocolates in the form of skulls, graves and death figures linked to celebrations of Mexico's All Souls' Day, or the hot cross buns that commemorate the Christian Passion.

Anthropologists ascribe the origin of edible toys to gifts dedicated to gods and spirits. Animal and human figures made of dough are explained as a type of sacrifice; their beginnings among Eastern Slavs have been traced to the 12th century. In that region they are usually linked with the service of holy communion. Some edible toys no doubt originated as food meant as a sacrifice to the dead. It seems that the production of cheese figures in 19th-century Galicia was connected with a rite honouring the dead. They were given to children as an inducement for them to pray for deceased members of the family.

Figural pastry has often played an important ritual role in the life of adults. The making, giving and consuming of it was associated with important occasions, for instance, with the celebration of individual saint's days in Bulgaria, or the celebration of the birth of a child, taking marriage vows, in services honouring the dead and rituals heralding the approach of spring. Figural pastry appears on the same occasions in Central Europe, including Poland, and in Russia. In Bohemia the form of the pastries was dictated by the following customs: for birthdays and vow-taking, wreaths, stars, deer and foxes; for weddings, two rings or wreaths, the figures of Adam and Eve, cradles, children and a pair of turtle doves; for honouring the dead, a snake, a lizard and a swan; for the spring festival, a lark, a swallow, an ox-drawn cart, a seed-drill barrow, and a seed basket.

Besides the religious symbolism, the sex of the child dictated the form of the gift. In Hesse in Germany, little boys were given figures of horseback riders, while girls received hearts, infants or dolls holding babies in their arms. The same practice is common in Hungary and Rumania. The figure on horseback as a boy's toy and the infant as a girl's toy are common throughout Europe.

Edible toys and figures made of gingerbread equally appear to be universal. They were generally modelled in wooden moulds into which the dough was poured and pressed. The finished, baked figures were then decorated, most often with icing sugar, but also by pasting on printed pictures or wrapping in tin foil. Icing tended to be replaced by pasted pictures in the late 19th century. The subjects were riders on horseback, infants, dolls with infants, hearts, soldiers, horse-drawn carriages, fish, baskets of flowers and figures in period costumes. Gingerbread cakes were sold at fairs on saint's days or other important religious holidays.

In Hesse pastries were baked and decorated with icing sugar for the first day of the New Year. Boys received riders on horses and girls were given hearts. This custom persisted until the end of the 1920s. Edible toys for New Year were also made in Lusatia.

Generally recognized symbols of spring's approach in the form of eggs and rabbits are connected with Easter. In addition to baked figures, on Easter Monday wooden, or clothed, or other types of rabbits appeared. Eggs, hard-boiled, or hollow with painted shells are among traditional Easter gifts in many parts of Europe. In Eastern and Southern Europe, particularly Russia, Rumania and Yugoslavia, the custom of giving festively decorative bread loaves and pastry buns to churches and to priests of the Orthodox Church has continued, and is unquestionably connected with gifts of buns and pastries to children. Figures of rabbits and ostriches made of dough are known in the Rhineland. In the Wallis Valley of Switzerland, dough figures were prepared for Easter in the shape of dolls. There were special Easter pastries in Bohemia and Bavaria, and in Poland confectioners prepared cocks, hares with a fish or a young

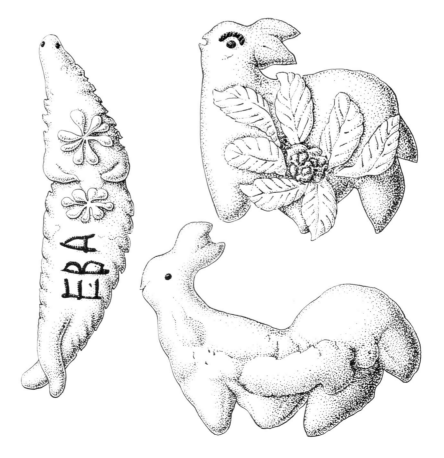

158   So-called Bread of the Dead. Mexico, before 1982. H. 34.5 cm, 17 cm and 16.5 cm. To this day the tradition has been maintained of baking these figural breads, especially in Oaxaca and Guerrero states of Mexico.

144

159 European figural bread:
(A) Sturgeon pressed into a mould (gingerbread). Gorodtse, Russia, 19th century.
(B) Hand-modelled horse and sledge of dough. Pacov, Bohemia, 19th century.
(C) Bread figures. Wallis canton, Switzerland, 19th century.

man between its paws, or fruits such as apples and mushrooms.

During Lent in 19th-century Moscow, gingerbread-makers brought their wares to open-air fairs from as far afield as Arkhangelsk. According to contemporary accounts, Tver gingerbread was the best. It came in the form of dogs, cocks, deer and generals on horseback.

In the post-Easter, spring period, people in Galicia paid tribute to the dead. For this occasion Hutsul women made figures of horses, horseback riders and sheep, modelled from cheese or curds. Some figures were offered in churches as remembrances of the dead, while others were given to children as gifts with the request that they pray for the souls of the dead. In the 1890s, in a number of villages of Galicia these items were still being made. To this day too the production of cheese and curd figures has continued sporadically in the Richka community, Ivano-Frankovsk district (Ukraine), and in the Tatra area of Poland. These same figures also appeared in the autumn, at All Souls' and All Saints'.

In the foothills of the Tatra Mountains, Czechoslovakia, after 1900, goat-cheese hearts and animals were pressed in wooden moulds, particularly in Slovakia and Poland where one- and two-part wooden moulds were used, for instance in the shape of a hen.

In Germany, gingerbread toys were linked with the start of the school year. It was the custom to give children going to school for the first time a baked blackboard with the alphabet on it, often decorated with figures of a teacher and pupils.

Another major occasion for figure pastries was All Souls'. In Europe this festival of the dead has a sombre character, but an entirely different atmosphere prevails in Central America and Mexico. Over the centuries after Christianity first came to that region, the festival was modified until it became essentially a folk celebration. The holiday of the dead is part of the holiday of life, in harmony with pre-Columbian Indian tradition. Therefore the most varied symbols of death, but in caricatured form, come as no surprise. Skulls and skeletons are produced in every im-

145

aginable way, and often adorned with the Christian name of the child to whom it is given. Smooth little sugar and chocolate children's graves, bright with colours and decorations, and their features enhanced still more by coloured paper and tin foil, are another jolly but macabre tradition. The children also receive sugar pigs, turkeys, lambs, and baskets of flowers and fruit. Figures of mermaids, fish and various other animals baked from white bread dough are also on sale.

Around St Martin's Day (November 11) and in Lent (February), when geese in Central Europe were fed bran mash, children used the same material to make pastries that looked like intertwined snakes. This custom has been confirmed in the area around Martin in Slovakia.

Many edible toys are linked to St Nicholas's Day, when they are or were given to children. They were often made at home, but today are more often bought. Besides figures of St Nicholas and devils, those of tiny people, animals and infants, or geometric pictures were baked from sweetened dough, sometimes with raisins and candied fruit. These are found in Czechoslovakia, Austria and southern Germany. Gingerbread makers prepared alphabets for this occasion and, according to surviving reports, the children took these 'sweet letters' to school: this tradition goes back to 17th-century Bohemia.

Also in Klatovy, Bohemia, during the pre-Christmas period, figures of animals, riders, wagons and carts with a team of horses were made from bread dough. In South Bohemian villages, around the town of Tábor, such figures were still being made at that time of the year until the Second World War. It was the custom in Bohemia to place these 'toy' buns in the coffins of children who died during Advent.

Figures made at home of dried fruit in the form of devils, chimney sweeps or dolls with a parasol or a muff, were also sold at St Nicholas fairs. These figures were not linked only to the St Nicholas holiday on December 6, but also at times to that of St Barbara (December 4) and St Lucy (December 13) when, according to local custom, children also received gifts.

Pastries and cakes in the form of figures are also associated with Christmas. In Swabia, until the end of the 19th century it was the custom to prepare for the Christmas Eve table figures representing genre scenes; these cakes were known as *Springerle*. In making them, the dough was pressed into a series of moulds carved in a large wooden board, so that it was possible to obtain 30 or 40 figures or groups in one batch. Moulds of this kind have been found dating from the 14th century.

In the 19th century, tragacanth figures achieved great popularity. Confectioners had produced them for children as early as the 17th century; even Comenius mentions them. They were made from a mixture of tragacanth gum, flower and sugar, with colouring added. Besides genre fig-

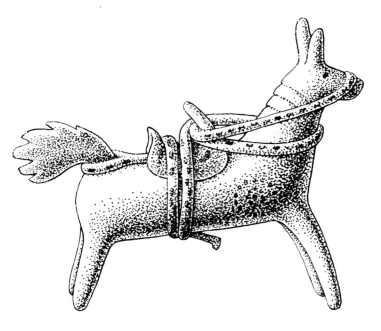

160   Horse modelled in cheese. Poland, mid-20th century. Such cheese horses are also known from the western Ukraine.

146

ures and all sorts of animals, figures of soldiers and portraits of military leaders such as Napoleon were made. Apart from individual figures, some furnishings for doll's houses were made from this composition for which the confectioners of Strasbourg were especially famous.

A number of figural edible toys, like gingerbread men, were made and sold throughout the year. But some pastry 'toys' were not edible. A good example is the figures produced, from about 1700 to 1900, in the Czech town of Pacov. Confectioners modelled individual figures in small moulds, then they were joined with soft dough or white of eggs, and sometimes even gum. The figures were coloured with the juice of elderberries, bilberries or other strongly coloured fruits; sometimes they were given added decoration consisting of a black outline and painted details with pieces of gold foil pasted on. Some were flat, intended to be looked at frontally, others were three-dimensional. Among the figures produced were forest animals, birds, devils and St Nicholas, dishes, horseback riders, a cobler working at his last and the carriages of the gentry.

Similar products were made at the same time in the Sonneberg area of Thuringia. Again the figures were not intended to be eaten as the flour was mixed with gum, and they were often formed in wooden moulds. These products, however, were the work of waxmakers, rather than bakers or confectioners.

On the borderline dividing pastry toys from those modelled in clay or plaster and other mixtures are several figural toys from Příbram in Bohemia. The dough was mixed with gum, sawdust or chalk. They were modelled mostly by hand and after being baked they were painted with bright colours, and sometimes lacquered. Some producers used wooden moulds of birds such as doves, hens, roosters and geese. The production of these figures is closely connected with cult objects, especially Nativity figures.

Only rarely has a traditionally made pastry toy survived to the present day. For instance, on the Polish side of the Tatra Mountains, in the district of Ostroleka, figures of animals are still being made. Nowadays, they must be considered an expression of folk art rather than children's toys, as are similar Moravian pastries of hand-modelled and cut-out figures of birds, etc.

Paper and Papier Mâché

Except in Asian countries, the history of paper and papier mâché hardly extends beyond 1900. At present, toys of this type are known only in Europe, Asia and America.

The basis of papier mâché figures, masks, helmets and other toys is always a mould. Judging from 16th-century German representations and accounts from 19th-century Russia, it would seem that an older type of mould was the model for the type used for this material. It was in this mould that the toy was modelled. In Asia and also in folk workshops in Mexico, a similar type of mould is used to the present day. It was made of wood or fired clay and before being used was greased or lacquered to prevent saturation by water. Older moulds no longer needed to be wiped because they were sufficiently impregnated with a protective grease. In making the toys, pieces of wet paper were pasted around the mould in layers until filled. After drying, the form was cut in two so that the mould could be removed. The two halves were then glued together and the surface decorated with paint or paper.

A later method of making papier mâché toys was in two negative plaster moulds into which several layers of soaked paper was pressed. After removal from the mould, the toy was hand-finished and glued together. The material used was predominantly cardboard or newspaper. The glues were made of tragacanth gum and a mixture of flour and water. After being painted the paper toys were usually varnished to improve their appearance and durability.

In Europe the oldest recorded example of the production of papier mâché objects is an engraving dating from the end of the 16th century, showing Nuremberg craftsmen at work. On the table are ready-made heads of dolls and the moulds from which they were made. The accompanying text explains that they are forming heads made of *Pappenzeuch*, or papier mâché. The text also explains that tragacanth gum was used as the paste. The question, of course, is to what extent the engraving depicts toymakers; most researchers incline to the view that the master craftsman in the picture is making figures for cult purposes of some kind.

In Sonneberg, the production of dolls of papier mâché was introduced as late as 1806. At that time, a previously unknown craft came into existence; the woodcarver and lathe operator working with wood and the modeller working with wax were replaced by the press operator. In Alpine centres, too, the making of toys of papier mâché was only introduced in the 19th century, and it is probable that papier mâché began to be used generally in European toymaking production from that period, although 18th-century examples are known.

In 19th-century England the dolls known as jumping jacks, often in harlequin dress, appeared, but most are of French or German origin.

Russian papier mâché toys, the first being dolls, began to be made in the first half of the 19th century in the village of Sergiev Posad, known today as Zagorsk. According to oral tradition, the first creator was inspired by the technique of gluing together alabaster crosses employed by monks in nearby Troitsky Monastery. In the early period the figures were made in three-dimensional wooden moulds, some of which are in the local toy museum. It was not until the 1860s that plaster was used, and Zagorsk remains the only centre of this technique in Russia. Toys with genre themes were also made, such as a carousel with saddled horses, a little girl

161 Baby doll, painted
papier mâché. Zagorsk,
Russia, before 1945.
H. 25 cm, w. 10.5 cm.

149

on a swing, children with lambs, swans and their young, boys riding a rooster, etc. Some toys were movable when wound up by a crank. Pairs of such movable figures are recorded: a little girl with a goat, a bear and goat and the figures of Bura and the Cossack. They were brightly painted, dressed in clothes of fabric or of other material pasted directly on to the figure.

In Bohemia in the second half of the 19th century candy boxes of papier mâché were designed as animals, some of which were adapted to specific demands.

For instance, at Easter these boxes appeared in the form of eggs, hens and hares. Dolls made from rolls of paper were also sold at fairs. The roll of paper served as the base on which the doll was modelled, before being wrapped in coloured paper and ribbons, or ruffled, coloured paper dresses draped around the base.

In Italy several centres made toys of papier mâché. Milan, where the production of wooden toys was also concentrated, was the most important, but other

162   Castle made of cardboard and printed paper. Erzgebirge, Bohemia, 1880s–1890s. The building and fortifications can be folded into a box which forms the 'base' of the castle. H. 22.5 cm, foundations 35 × 25 cm.

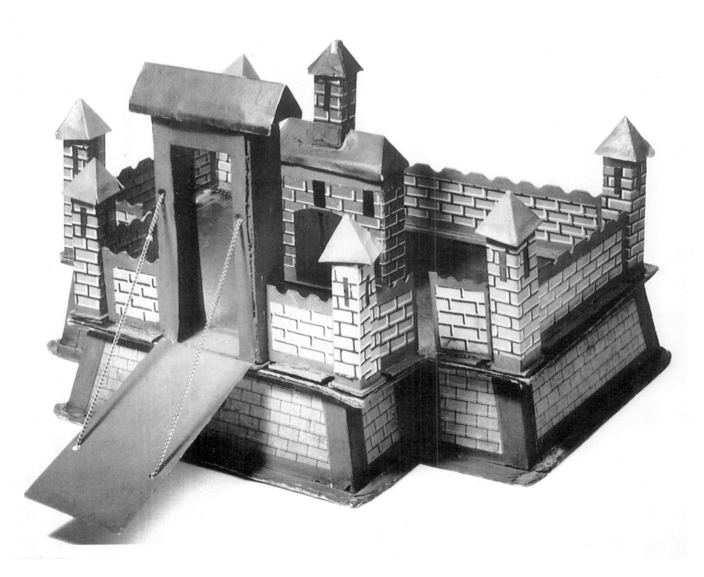

163   Driver, buggy and horse, painted
paper and wood. Zagorsk, Russia, before
1945. H. 13 cm, l. 22 cm.

workshops existed in Naples, Cremona
and the town of Lecce, whence came multicoloured genre figures of famous rob-
bers and their companions, and carica-
tures of the inhabitants of different regions, such as a Neapolitan eating macar-
oni, were popular. In Sweden the figure of
a reindeer made of papier mâché is recorded, although nothing is known of its
makers.

In addition to dolls and dolls heads,
castles and fortresses were made of cardboard and paper in the 19th century. In
boys' games, the fortresses were attacked
by wooden or tin soldiers. These were
made all over Europe and in America, but

they differ architecturally, in accordance
with local traditions, and sometimes in the
way they were made. Some fortresses
were conceived in the round, whereas
others were intended only to be viewed
from the front with a flat section behind
like a backdrop. These distinctions also
apply to contemporary, factory-made
versions.

Cardboard houses painted and covered
with mica from the Erzgebirge date from
the end of the 19th century or the beginning of the 20th. They are known too in
the Kralice district of north-eastern Bohemia, where production of paper Nativity scenes was popular. Very small ver-

sions were used as hanging ornaments on Christmas trees and as toys.

In the second half of the 19th century paper figures were made both at home and in factories throughout Europe and the United States. In shape and size they were similar to tin figures. They were pasted on either side with printed coloured paper and most were fastened to wooden bases. Thematically too they were related to tin figures — marketplaces with stallkeepers and customers, forest animals and hunters, a circus with exotic animals and gaping spectators, and many soldiers. These paper figures, like tin soldiers, are somewhere on the borderline between a folk and an elite toy, but they were sold in large numbers to ordinary people.

Among European paper toys, certain others should be mentioned: the rolled-up paper whistles and the 'raspberry' blowers bought at country fairs and open-air markets, and the accordion books and other early 'novelty' picture books, which often incidentally provide a guide to the content of folklore in their country of origin.

Some German accordion books of the second half of the 19th century are of special interest to collectors, though not strictly to be classed as folk toys since they were, of course, commercially produced. On the linked pages they displayed pictures of, say, animals in the zoo, circus scenes, a forest scene, and so on.

The first printed cut-out dolls made their appearance over half a century earlier: probably the first book of this type was printed in 1791. Allied items, known from pre-Victorian times, are puzzles like jigsaw puzzles, various board games (horse-racing furnished a popular motif) and puzzles of other kinds.

Papier mâché toys are much more familiar in parts of Asia than they are in Europe, and probably originated in China.

In India, the production of papier mâché toys probably began at the beginning of the 19th century. During the past 150 years, workshops have come into existence in Lucknow, Madras and Junagadh in Gujarat, where dolls and genre figures are made. Workshops in several other large cities, for instance Bombay, Calcutta and Delhi, directed their attention mainly to costumed dolls, which are now, in fact, typically souvenir items.

Costumed souvenir figures of folded paper are made in Rajasthan, and there are workshops producing similar objects in Amritsar and the Punjab.

A different kind of product comes from Orissa, where the workshops produced brightly painted figures of animals, some of which have an unusual shape — for instance, two-headed antelopes. There are movable toys also, frequently with pendulum-swinging heads, most often the figure of a tiger. Miniature cult masks and figures of local gods are produced. Masks of papier mâché intended for children's games were also made in Nepal.

Workshops processing papier mâché are found in Thailand's large cities. The toys are modelled on a core of unbaked clay, which is removed after the papier mâché has hardened. Besides dolls, elephants were popular figures, the painting of their bodies resembling the historical trapping of elephants used by Thailand's rulers. Papier mâché toys are invariably lacquered throughout south-east Asia.

From Burma come reports of dolls and animal figures such as tigers, as well as a great variety of military helmets or hats of monks and courtiers that are replicas of historical models.

Although China is the ancient homeland of paper and papier mâché toys there is virtually no information about production. However, in papier mâché and in other forms of processed paper the same subject-matter appears as in wooden or pottery toys. Paper 'dragons' have already been mentioned; a variant is the large three-dimensional kite carried by children in processions. There are also accordion books with three-dimensional pop-up scenes.

The Japanese learned the technique of papier mâché from the Chinese, perhaps in the Muromachi period (1336—1573). Toys of this material are recorded from the mid-17th century. They are still modelled in exactly the same way today, in wooden moulds with moist sheets of paper which are pasted together. After drying, the toy is cut into two halves, the mould removed and the paper 'skin' pasted together again, painted and sometimes lacquered. The best known of such toys are tigers with movable heads, masks in the form of lion's heads and figures of *Daruma*. While the tigers are pure entertainment, the others have religious links

152

164 Dolls, painted papier mâché. Coyoacán,
Mexico, before 1982. H. 68 cm and 53 cm.

165 Tiger and the monkey Sun Wu-k'ung,
painted and lacquered ceramic. China,
before 1965. Sun Wu-k'ung is the
principal hero of folk tales about the journey
of the monk Hsuan-tsang to India in
629-645. H. 2 cm and 4 cm.

166   Child with a pomegranate, painted
ceramic. China, before 1965. The
pomegranate is the symbol of the wish to
have many sons in the family. H. 10.5 cm,
w. 10 cm.

167   Pagoda, and bridge with tower,
porcelain with enamel. Workshops in
Wing-dao, China, 1950s. H. pagoda 5.2 cm,
bridge 4.7 cm.

168   Sugar toys and delicacies for the All Souls' Day festival. Michoacán, Mexico, before 1982. Besides the pig, turkey and vegetable basket there is also a miniature grave. H. 7—9.2 cm, grave 13.5 × 5.5 cm.

169   Jigsaw puzzle from the end of the 19th
century, printed paper, Germany. Jigsaw
puzzles have been available at toy markets
from the first half of the 19th century to the
present day. 23 × 16.5 cm.

170   Miniature monk's hat of papier
mâché. Rangoon, Burma, before 1969.
H. 22 cm, d. 27 cm.

171 Elephant with nodding head carrying
a Chinese child with a fan, painted papier
mâché. Kyü-shü Island, Japan, 1970s. An
example of toys depicting unknown animals
and unknown nations in somewhat
distorted form. H. 19 cm, l. 24 cm.

172 Market place, cardboard and printed paper. Bohemia, end of 19th century. The figures can be viewed from front and back; the subject matter comes from popular tin figures. H. adults 8 cm, children 6.2 cm, stalls 9.2 cm.

and are probably among the oldest of Japanese toys. The lion's dance, performed by adults at New Year and at other holidays, was supposed to chase away all sorts of evil powers and catastrophes from people and their dwellings. The miniaturization of masks converted a cult item into a toy. It is interesting to note that the ritual dance of the dancing lion came to Japan from China and the lion was called the 'Chinese dog'. Figures of *Daruma* depict the Indian monk Bodhidharma who sat for years engrossed in meditation until his legs became stunted. According to tradition this monk brought to China the teaching of Zen. He is traditionally shown in male form, but a variation is a young girl, this form being made in workshops in Kanazawa, Ishikawa prefecture, and in the prefecture of Ehime. Figures of *Daruma* are considered to be symbols of happiness, success and good living. Some do not have eyes and the owner paints them in when he approaches with a wish. The figures were made throughout Japan, but

173 Raspberry blowers made of printed paper are among classic items sold at open-air fairs. These were found in Bohemia in the 1970s, but they were also known in Japan in the 19th century. L. 36 cm.

161

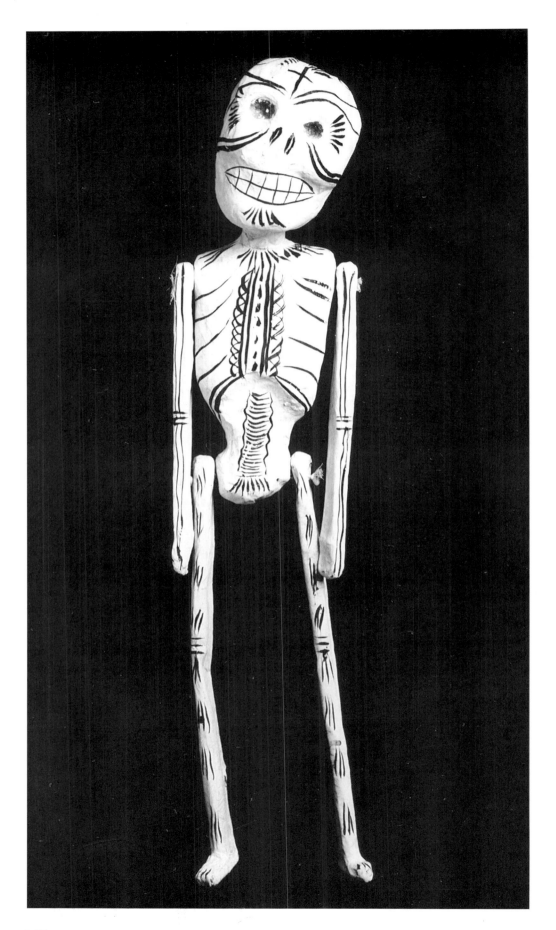

174   Figure of Death, the Grim Reaper, the 'calavera', painted papier mâche. Celaya, Mexico, before 1982. 'Calavera' prints are sold during the All Saints' Day holiday. H. 78 cm.

like wooden toys they are sometimes linked to religious sites; for instance, one characteristic figure is produced in the area around the temple in Takasaki.

In addition to paper lion masks, there are masks representing demons or caricaturing individual human types. The best such masks are, perhaps, from the Tosa area of Shikoku Island.

Besides religious objects, there are figural toys that draw on secular subject, portraits of famous dancers or similar heroes of love stories. There are also many animal figures, of which the most sought-after are made on Shikoku Island, where tigers, oxen and buffaloes carrying loads of rice, the symbol of happines and success at the New Year, are made.

One of the most important centres of papier mâché toys is Fukushima prefecture. The towns of Miharu and Takashiba are renowned for their workshops where at the beginning of the 19th century several thousand kinds of papier mâché toys were produced. The workshops concentrated in Tokyo and surrounding districts also enjoy a great tradition: among typical toys is the figure known as the 'eastern dog'.

Although today the production of papier mâché toys has spread to many places, in the past it was concentrated in royal towns of the individual Japanese principalities, where the princes encouraged toymaking, and in areas where paper was produced.

In Japan, painted and folded paper toys were manufactured professionally. Great favourites are the *anesama* dolls from Shimane prefecture, but workshops making these dolls exist in other parts of the country too. At the Boys' Festival, May 5, they also make kites with painted decoration and printed figures and streamers in the shape of carp, hung on poles near houses where small children live. In Japan as in other Far Eastern countries, the carp is a symbol of strength and endurance. During the 18th century paper was employed for the bodies of *hina* dolls associated with the Girls' Festival, but the head and arms, perhaps oddly, were of wood.

At the beginning of the 20th century, paper figures were made in Japan in which, by pulling a string, the eyes and a tongue could be made to move.

Folk production of toys in the Americas is most significant in Mexico. Although its products in pre-Columbian times were made of something similar to paper, the production of papier mâché toys started only at the end of the 18th century. In some areas it was introduced by Europeans only after the Second World War. Celaya in Guanajuato is one of the outstanding centres of traditional production, with its miniature masks designed for children, its dolls with movable arms and legs, figural whistles, and figures that are ceremonially burnt during Easter celebrations.

Another production centre is Cordoba, where sound-emitting toys are made of papier mâché combined with wood and other materials. Shirring grasshoppers are produced in the capital, Mexico City, as well as pinwheels, paper kites and papier mâché balls.

Papier mâché boxes for sweets, shaped like animals such as bulls, which are produced in a workshop in Tucson, Arizona, are evidently drawn from the Spanish colonial tradition. Filled with gifts and sweets they are hung from the ceiling of a room on birthdays or at Christmas and the children, using sticks, try to get the sweets out of the baskets.

Other Materials

Besides wood and clay, folk toys, especially those made with a market in mind, employed a great variety of other materials, such as stone, glass, wax or ivory (although the latter is rather rare), as well as metals, like lead and tin, which are easily worked.

Both amateur and professional makers made use of these materials, and of others, more ephemeral, which were the by-products of agricultural processes: straw, leaves, moss, bast, reeds, etc.

In England home-made dolls fashioned from jute, flax and straw are usually linked to ancient agricultural ceremonies, although the craft tradition cannot be traced further back than the 17th century. In agricultural areas of East Anglia and the West County people continued to make these dolls in the early decades of this century. The centre of the straw-plaiting industry, however, was Luton. The Luton workers occasionally made straw dolls as well as the hats and baskets that were their bread and butter. One example was a flower girl which perhaps drew on the pedlar dolls that were great favourites around the mid-19th century.

On the continent of Europe, the making of straw toys was still widespread at the beginning of the 20th century, but surviving examples of dolls or baskets are only to be seen today in folk museums, the odd trendy country shop or private collections.

Among the oldest straw toys are 18th-century figures from Venice dressed in carnival costumes. Similar figures were made in other parts of northern Italy in the second half of the 19th century.

From northern Europe, especially Sweden, there are sets of human and animal folk figures plaited from natural and coloured straw. These include horses, goats, men and women in folk costumes, sometimes in pairs, and angels. A special role in the folk tradition is the straw kid (goat) known as *Jul Bock*. Children believed he brought Christmas presents and *Jul Bock* figures, ranging in size from a few centimetres to a couple of metres, were placed under Christmas trees. It is possible that the *Jul Bock* kid is connected with the mythical spirit known as *jultomte* who appears during the pre-Christmas period accompanying Saint Lucy. Kids, Nativity scenes and angels were made in various sizes, all of straw, bound together with red thread, the colour being regarded as the symbol of life. These traditional Nordic toys were originally produced only by amateurs, but by the end of the 19th century the market supported a healthy commercial output.

There is evidence of the existence of straw dolls from Russia, the Moscow region especially, but little from the rest of Europe. Straw goats, horses and other animals are known in Yugoslavia and straw dolls were produced professionally in Germany, for instance in the Magdeburg area where figures of costumed couples have survived.

The Far East, more specifically China and South-East Asia, is a more promising region for plaited toys. They are primarily animals made of strips of palm leaves. They are left in the natural colour of the material, painted with a simple geometric pattern, or the whole figures are painted. Besides palm leaves, straw and other grasses are used.

Although little is known of the craft in India, brightly coloured straw figures were made in Bihar. Chiefly souvenirs today, in earlier times they were wedding gifts or were used as cult objects. In Bengal miniature tools such as grain scoops were made.

In Thailand, straw carp are hung over

175 Page from a German accordion book about a visit to the circus, coloured print on paper. The book contains scenes from the circus ring with glimpses into the circus menagerie. Second half of the 19th century. Size of page 33.5 × 22.5 cm.

the beds of little children. The manner in which they are hung recalls the European use of wooden and straw doves over children's beds or cradles. The Thai carp are usually painted green, sometimes gilded. The popularity of the carp motif results from the Far Eastern tradition of admiration for the persistence, strength and other manly qualities of this fish.

Figures of animals made of palm leaves, such as turtles, fish and buffaloes (some on wood bases with wheels), are known from Indonesia, where young girls plaited Sagus palm-leaf dolls. The children of Sumatra made painted masks for their games, representing various animals, such as cats, tigers and monkeys. On the island of Mentawai, near Sumatra, pinwheels were made of coconut leaves.

Baskets made of coloured straw and decorated with different coloured enamels come from China. Three-dimensional as well as flat animals are also produced, for example the panda, little horses, birds and frogs. Some miniature palm-leaf figures, usually stiffened with enamel, are attached to a whistle and fastened with string to a wooden handle. A whistling sound is produced when they are spun around.

Stylized human figures enlivened the children's world of several Siberian ethnic groups and some 19th-century figures from the Gold people of Russia have been preserved.

Little straw horses and other Japanese animals are, according to some researchers, the oldest, most 'traditional' Japanese folk toys. Especially popular in Nagano, they appear in other areas as well, for example, in Iwate prefecture in Tohoku region. In these territories, the local people believed that the horses carry the local gods, especially the god of the fields, on their backs, and they are therefore connected with agricultural cults and placed on altars. Nevertheless, they are also used as children's toys, notably during harvest celebrations. Although they can be bought, the tradition of their being made at home continues. Sometimes there is a stylized figure of a samurai sitting on a horse, a gift for a boy whose parents wish for the child the skill, strength and honour of the samurai; often these are known historical personalities whose name is written on the banner the figure carries.

In the United States, plaited toys have survived only sporadically. Examples are the dolls made at the beginning of this century by basket-makers of the Papago and other ethnic groups from the Columbia River basin. The technique used is the same employed by basketmakers, and the figures are dressed in European clothes, sometimes wearing a hat. Plaited figures of Indians of several Arizona tribes were also made. Miniature models of children's papooses of various sizes are frequently seen in museums; they originated in California and Nevada. Whether they were made originally as toys is uncertain, but the children of European colonists used them as such.

The production of straw toys persisted in Latin American countries, notably Mexico. From the state of Pueblo there are figures of mules loaded with goods, usually accompanied by horseback riders. The figures are often stiffened with sticks or reeds, and are brightly painted. From the state of Michoacán come flat figures of *caballeros* in sombreros, horseback riders, acrobats and musicians, which are plaited from blades of reeds or wheat straw, and sometimes from strips of palm leaves; occasionally the makers combined all three materials. One of the Michoacán centres of production is the town of Pátzcuaro, where two kinds of lake reeds are used to make toys. In this same region, the toymakers of Toluca prefer to combine reeds with palm leaves. Michoacán figures are left outdoors until the straw turns a deep yellow. Three-dimensional genre figures of villagers in big straw hats or

176　Masks made of painted palm leaves. Central Sumatra, Indonesia, early 20th century.

177 Married farm couple, coloured straw. Sweden, 1930s. H. 40 cm.

horseback riders are among the favourite toys in the state of Sonora. Other centres making straw figures of angels and animals, as well as rattles of coloured straw and grasses, are also found in the states of Hidalgo and Guanajuato.

In Bolivia and Peru miniature reed boats are made, similar to those still to be seen on Lake Titicaca. They usually have sails, but sometimes only a paddle and occasionally the figure of an Indian. Origin-ally toys for the local children, these models are now sold to tourists as souvenirs. Miniature baskets and straw figures were made in the mountainous areas of Bolivia.

Toys were made from reeds in many other parts of the world. For example, the rack wagon and the pair of draught animals pulling a cart come from Switzerland. Reed dolls, sometimes with ingenious moving parts, are made in Zaire, the Congo and Cameroon.

178   Basket with lid,
painted and lacquered straw.
China, before 1965.
H. 9 cm, w. 10.7 cm.

179   Tortoise on wheels,
palm leaves with painting.
Java, Indonesia, before
1945. L. 37 cm, w. 16 cm.

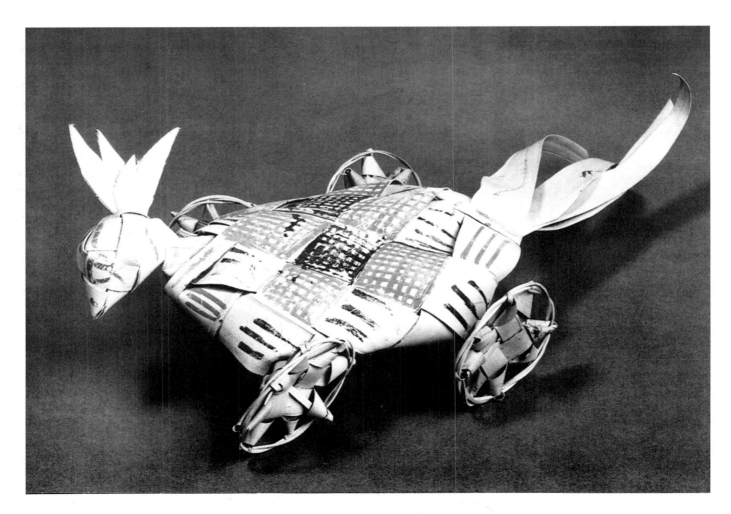

180   Woven straw basket.
China, before 1965.
H. 15 cm.

181   Panda and horse,
plaited palm fibres. China,
before 1965. H. horse
10.5 cm, panda 11.5 cm.

169

182 Bengalese straw-woven miniature basket of the type used to winnow rice. Before 1960. L. 10.7 cm, w. 10 cm.

them is simple: the husked and dried leaves are rolled up to form the body of the figure and the narrow ends of the stalks are used for the arms and legs. The body is wrapped in flatter leaves to form the clothes. In recent times these dolls have become the object of tourists' and collectors' interest, which explains why a number of originally amateur producers now devote themselves intensively to their manufacture.

In Bohemia and Moravia today not only are individual straw figures plaited but genre or Nativity scenes are made entirely of this material.

In the United States the first growers of maize and the first makers of corn dolls were Indians, particularly the eastern nations. The Iroquis to this day earn extra cash by plaiting very realistic traditional figures. Farther west, female figures in

Not surprisingly, the Amazon basin is a region where the materials offered by the forest are widely employed in toymaking. Both adults and children make figures of birds, animals such as tortoises, armadillos, jaguars, etc. and fish. Toys made by tribes living near the Xingu River of Brazil are often found in private and museum collections.

Maize husks were already mentioned above. To make various figures from

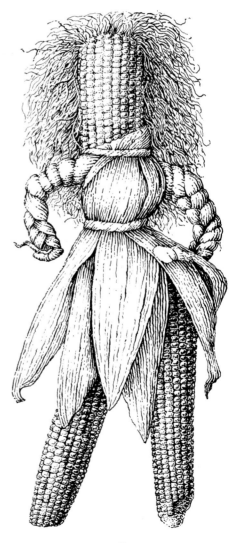

183 (A) Thai doll of dried maize husks, 20th century. Perhaps such dolls came into existence under the influence of missionaries. Dolls are usually wooden there.
(B) Mexican doll made from maize ear and dried maize husks, 20th century.

A

B

184 Miniature baskets, split osiers. Bolivia, before 1937. H. 8.5 cm and 9.5 cm.

185 Turtle, duck and kitten, coloured raffia palm fibres. Ibibio, Nigeria, before 1968. H. turtle 9.5 cm, kitten 15.5 cm, duck 9 cm.

187 Basket, plaited and painted split osiers with the souvenir inscription 'Helsingborg-Minne-Frán-1905'. Sweden, 1905. H. 13 cm.

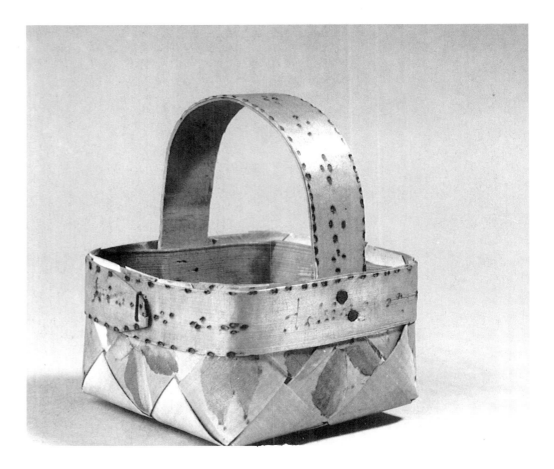

186 Stylized doll of plaited grass with metal earrings, necklace and draped fabric skirt. Tanzania, second half of 19th century. Millet stalks can be used instead of grass.

188 Rattle, plaited and painted split osiers. Crimean Tatars, Simferopol, Ukraine, before 1899. H. 8 cm.

189 Figure of a 'muzhik' of moss and pine cones, so-called *mokhovnik*. Russia, 19th century.

modern dress are more likely to be encountered. The 19th-century pioneers of the West used to fashion figures from the cobs, which are of course sufficiently durable to make tobacco pipes.

The soft, shaggy animals made in eastern Nigeria introduce another organic material, raffia bast. There are six types of raffia palm in tropical Africa, and the leaves as well as the firm, fibrous bast of all of them provide material for weaving clothes, making rugs and other fabric. Among the Ibo, raffia is used to make animals for children, the natural colour of the raffia being combined with other, coloured fibres. Today these animals are sold in most Nigerian cities, having been purchased in the villages of their origin by travelling middlemen.

In northern Liberia young boys make swords, spears and imitation rifles from the leaves of palms and similar plants. From strips of palm leaves they weave a toy called a 'hand-catcher'. It takes the form of a pliable cylinder, whose size can be reduced or increased by pressure. A hand thrust into the cylinder can thus be 'caught'.

At Troitskoe in Russia, figures are made from pine cones and dried moss. The common type is of a young boy with a stick, probably deriving from Russian fairy tales.

Birch bark is another rather unusual toymaking material. Dolls were sometimes made from it in Russia and Sweden, where the birch is a very common tree.

Basketmakers who weave their baskets from osiers (willow) would seem to be likely toymakers, though in fact examples are uncommon. Basket-weavers used a variety of other materials, including thin wooden strips and even creepers like ivy, and depending on the locality they also plaited objects of straw. In Croatia in the 19th century shepherds used to make baskets and other plaited objects, and basket-making was widely practised as a part-time activity in many areas.

Since finds of basket-woven toys are so few, it is impossible to gauge the ability or output of any individual craftsman or to classify his output by the types produced. Much depended on knowledge and skill, but sets of different types of basket were probably common, as the set made in a Saxon workshop in Lauter, near Zwickau, testifies. Customers there were able to choose from eight kinds of baskets for little girls to play with. Not only did the baskets differ in shape but also in decoration and price.

Toys made of large, hard-skinned vegetables like the gourd form another group, and examples exist throughout the world. We have already mentioned the Jack-o' Lantern masks made from a hollowed-out pumpkins which children in the United States use on Halloween. This custom has recently, as a result of American influence, become more popular in Europe, though of course it was from Europe that it emanated in the first place.

In China and Vietnam dried vegetable marrows were carved and decorated as baby's rattles, little dishes and figurines. Calabash dolls were widely made in East Africa, and were an important compo-

190 Dolls of birch bark. Sweden, 19th century. Birch bark was also used throughout Northern Europe to make boxes.

173

191 Calabash decorated doll with the engraved signature of its maker; the upper part, suggesting the head, has human hair. Zaramo tribe, Tanzania, 1944—47.

nent of the inititation ceremonies of girls. Calabash balls and dolls are also made in South Africa. In West Africa not only dolls but other toys were made of sections of calabash. The Indians in Mexico and tropical South America also used this material, which has the useful qualities of light weight and a hard surface that can be painted or varnished.

Wax appears sporadically in folk or ethnic toymaking. Wax dolls were first produced in Europe in the 18th century but were relatively a commercial product, intended chiefly for middle- or upper-class children and priced beyond the reach of peasants or workers. Between 1800 and 1850 Indian craftsmen in Mexico made wax dolls, under the influence of Spanish and Creole settlers, for whose children the toys were intended. Indian fighters in full dress were also made; although a rarity today, they were already on the borderline between toys and souvenirs.

Children themselves modelled wax figures. For instance, children on Luzon Island in the Philippines made pigs and human figures of wax, as did children of the forest tribes in the Amazon basin. Similar modelling was done in West Africa, in Senegal, Mali and Cameroon. In the second half of the 19th century, wax figures or heads of devils turned up at St Nicholas markets in Central Europe, competing with the plaster and paper equivalents. For the most part red or red and black wax was used.

In Chapter Two we mentioned toys made of fur and hide. Such dolls, singly or in pairs, were placed in children's papooses or on sledges throughout the area from Lapland to eastern Siberia. Besides the dolls, clothing for dolls was made from animal skin, for instance by some Siberian tribes.

Tin and lead toys are mostly confined to Europe, the first mention of moulded tin toys coming from Nuremberg in 1578. Cast figures, however, go back much further. Isolated examples of figures of knights on horseback have been found in France dating from about 1500. In the 16th century tin was used in Nuremberg along with wax, iron and wood, but large-scale production of tin soldiers as we know them today developed only in the 18th century. Their beginnings are linked with the name of Andreas Hilpert who, after moving to Nuremberg, simplified production by introducing shallow moulds. Hilpert made genre figures of people, animals with engraved Latin names for educational purposes and garden scenes which were signed 'A.H.', but the production of tin soldiers in particular perhaps owes more to his relative, Josef Gottfried Hilpert, who in 1775 produced 40 types of soldiers of the army of King Frederick the Great of Prussia; the number soon increased to 110. Later, soldiers occupied an important place in the output of all workshops specializing in tin figures, whether representing Napoleon's army or the soldiers of the First World War. Their popularity was reflected in Andersen's fairy tale about the brave tin soldier.

Production expanded from Nuremberg to other places, and in 1790 there were

192 Fur dolls. Chukchi, Siberia, Russia, early 20th century. Similar types are known from the Enisei River basin. Reindeer skin in particular was used to make these dolls. H. 14 cm and 13 cm.

193 Soldiers in French Army uniforms, painted tin. Germany, end of 19th century. H. 7.3 cm.

194 Tin figure of a knight. Found in the River Seine, France, 13th century. One of the oldest examples of tin toys. A few lead toys have survived, for instance a little armchair from the Roman period (*c.* 1st century B.C.).

casting workshops in Fürth: after 1800 they were set up in Berlin, Lüneburg and Wurttemberg, but the Nuremberg producers continued to set the style. In 1848 the firm of Heinrichsen introduced the so-called Nuremberg scale: 30 mm for infantry, 40 mm for cavalry. Recognized internationally only in 1924, the scale was adhered to by many firms much earlier.

Fürth was not the only Bavarian centre of tin toys. In the 1790s workshops sprang up in several small towns, for instance in Diessen and Landsberg, some of which have maintained their existence to the present day. In Diessen they continue to cast vases of flowers and all sorts of genre scenes, such as processions, pastoral idylls, or a married couple sitting down to eat. Miniature devotional articles are made, particularly tin communion plates and figures of Jesus and the saints. The tin workers traditionally reacted quickly to important events: around 1835, inspired by the new railway line between Nuremberg and Fürth, the first toy trains in tin appeared.

Saxon tin production began as late as 1800, the oldest centre being the town of Freiberg. Saxon toys drew on Nuremberg models and among the early examples are soldiers in the uniforms of the Napoleonic wars. Around 1850 Saxony produced a typical local tin toy — a miner, or miners taking part in processions and miners' galas. Genre scenes were also made, such as market stall-holders, street scenes and

circus performances. There were other Saxon workshops in Meissen and Grossenhain.

In the rest of Germany, mention should be made of other tin workshops which were renowned in the second half of the 19th century. Hildesheim specialized in costumed figures, animals and trees, while in Lübeck many types of soldiers and doll's cutlery sets were made.

The original stone moulds engraved with figures in low relief into which the molten metal was poured were later replaced by deeper moulds which produced more genuinely three-dimensional figures. Compared to the flat figures, these represented considerable progress. When painted and assembled according to type, they were packed in punnets. German tin toy centres controlled the continental European market for centuries. As well as current armies, they made historical tin soldiers such as Romans or crusaders fighting the Saracens.

Some European workshops managed to break the German monopoly on tin toy production, and in Switzerland there were workshops in Aarau famous for their representations of the participants in folk festivals. Paris had workshops by the end of the 18th century and Parisian lead figures of alloyed antimony from the C.B.G. company offered strong competition in the 19th century to German toys because they weighed less.

In most European countries tin pro-

195 Chinese kaleidoscope, printed paper and coloured glass, decorated on the outside with the motif of the god of longevity, two boys and a carp. Before 1956. Similar types were sold in Europe in the 19th century at open-air fairs. H. 16 cm.

196   Horse, painted papier mâché. Mexico
City, Mexico, before 1982. Based on
European models of hobby-horses.
H. 43 cm, l. 25 cm.

197   Skull of painted papier mâché intended
for All Souls' Day holiday. Mexico City,
Mexico, before 1982. H. 25.5 cm, w. 18 cm.

198   The Grim Reaper, painted papier
mâché. Mexico City, Mexico, before 1982.
The death motif — 'calavera' — played a big
part in the 19th century and first decades of
the 20th century in folklore and in political
satire. The motif of horror in Mexico is part
of the folk outlook on the world. H. 24.5 cm
and 26 cm.

199 Figure of an American Indian made of plaited plant roots. Arizona or New Mexico area, U.S.A., 1920s. Local basketmakers plait flasks and baskets in the same way. H. 26.5 cm.

200 Mounted rider and beast of burden,
painted straw, maize husks and wood. Santa
Maria de Chigmecatitlán, Mexico, before
1982. Rider h. 22 cm, l. 13 cm, donkey
h. 24.5 cm, w. 14 cm.

201   Painted tin figures — part of an
'English Hunt'. Nuremberg, Germany, 19th
century. H. 1 cm, 3 cm and 4 cm.

202   Carp, coloured fabric. China, before
1956. Popular subjects of cloth animal
figures are tigers, camels and horses.
H. 10 cm, l. 25 cm.

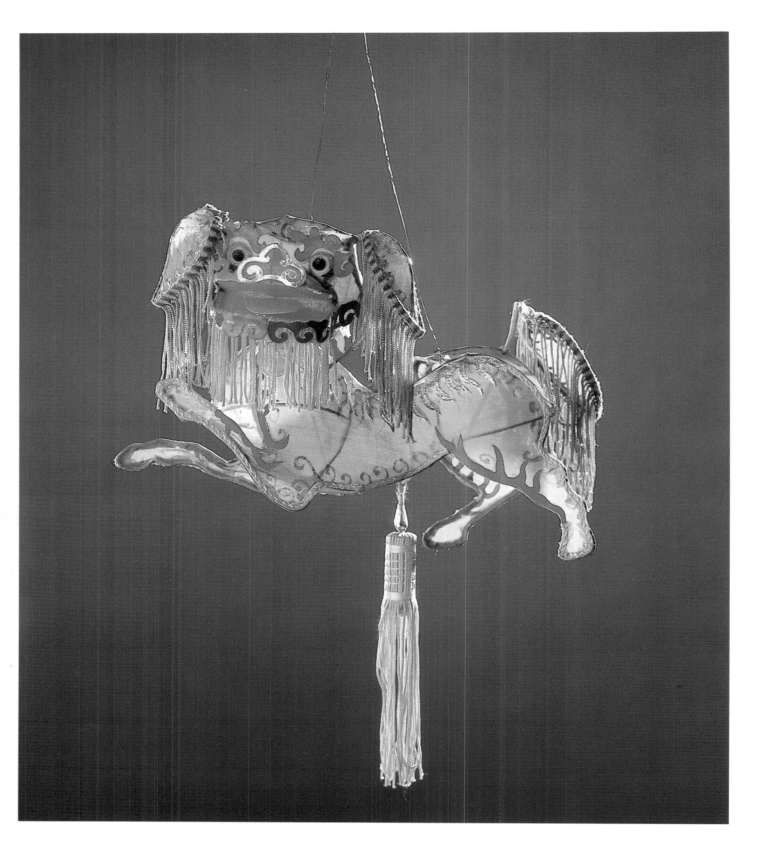

203   Chinese lantern shaped like a lion, silk
on wired frame. China, before 1965.
Chinese silk lanterns in the shape of crabs and
rats are also found. H. 11 cm, l. 16.5 cm.

184

204 Figure of a llama, limestone. La Paz, Bolivia, 1910. Stone figures for casting spells are sometimes grouped to form a square. Miniature skulls also appear among them. H. 4.5 cm, l. 5.2 cm.

duction only became established in the second half of the 19th century. A landmark was the opening of William Britain's factory in England in 1868. Besides the famous soldiers, Britain's also made cowboys and Indians, historical personalities, figures of well-known actors and singers, toy dishes, flower baskets and locomotives and rolling stock. The range of work was considerable, and so was productivity in the factory. In about 1900 one female worker could cast about 2,500 small tin figures in a single shift.

Not every country could survive German competition. Tin workshops set up to make toys in Russia in the 19th century all failed in time, due to the grip of imports on the domestic market.

Tin soldiers were cast for a time in Příbram, Bohemia, though the main output was of lead ornaments. (Early tin soldiers, though made of tin, were often called 'lead'.) Tin playthings were a secondary consideration for Czech workshops before 1850, although toys were produced occasionally as early as the 18th century. Apart from soldiers, various other figures — Indians, Arabs, etc. — similar to those from other European manufacturers were made. Only in the second half of the 19th century did a Brno manufacturer specialize in toys exclusively.

There was much less activity in southern Europe, although the tin works at Udine in Italy deserve a mention.

Cast metal toys were also produced on a more or less amateur basis, though as a means to make money. In Slovakia, for example, in the first decades of the 20th century, soldiers brought tin soldiers for their younger brothers in the villages, and the local craftsmen made moulds from them and cast copies in lead.

Among the few instances of cast toys outside Europe are the lead figures of animals which children in India received during celebrations dedicated to the goddess Kali. The figures were made in Calcutta in the second half of the 19th century.

Small tinned dishes, made in workshops that produced ornamental objects, can be included among metal toys. They were hand-made in Europe in the 18th and early 19th centuries, but later replaced by factory manufacture.

Brass miniatures of waterpots and other vessels, wrought, cast or made by other techniques, were produced in India, where brass dishes are a traditional feature of village households. Small brass dishes were also made in other parts of Asia, North Africa and South America.

In Mexico, besides miniature dishes and a great variety of tools and cutlery, human skulls and skeletons were and still are produced from tin. These miniatures are usually painted and arranged on glass shelves in small cabinets, to the delight of children.

It was only during the 20th century that wire toys appeared. Locally made cars, carts and animal figures are made in Afri-

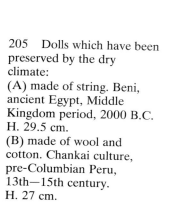

205 Dolls which have been preserved by the dry climate:
(A) made of string. Beni, ancient Egypt, Middle Kingdom period, 2000 B.C. H. 29.5 cm.
(B) made of wool and cotton. Chankai culture, pre-Columbian Peru, 13th—15th century. H. 27 cm.

206 Figure of a magician, fabric, painted
face. Made by Hausa women in Tripoli,
Libya, 1880. It belongs to a set of toys
representing a fakir, doctor, ruler and
women of different social classes. H. 6.7 cm,
max. w. 5.5 cm.

187

207   Brass containers — miniature dish for water and a box with a lid. India, before 1878. H. 3.3 cm and 5.5 cm.

ca, particularly in Tanzania, Togo and Ghana. Children themselves use this accessible material, though the wires may be plaited for them by adults.

Glass is the medium associated with a small but important group of toys. Among the oldest glass toys are marbles, made since the 19th century. Chiefly a European phenomenon, they are made in innumerable patterns and colours, utilizing most of the many decorative techniques of glass workers.

Blown glass figures of humans and animals were sold or given to customers and visitors at the glassworks. Subjects included human figures, devils, genre and hunting scenes, blown dishes, saucers, vases and jugs. Such a practice was widespread at larger glassworks in Bohemia, Germany, Mexico and elsewhere. From the history of the Lauscha glassworks in Germany we learn that glass figures are a relatively recent product. The works were established in the 16th century but

208   Rag dolls from Bihar, India, 20th century. H. of second pair 7 cm and 9 cm.

188

209 This cyclist on a two-wheeler was acquired in Harare, Zimbabwe, in 1989. It indicates the beginning of souvenir products based on children's toys. H. of figure on bicycle 21 cm.

only began making these small items and toys after 1820. The catalogue for 1831 offers figures of birds, deer, dogs, goats, hares, and also horseback riders and hunting scenes. In the mid-19th century these toys formed an important product of Sonneberg toymakers even in the context of overall exports, and in the 1870s they were exported to Britain and the United States as Christmas tree decorations. Glass toys are among those toys which bridge all social classes, and they also appeal to adults.

Connected with glass production are kaleidoscopes in which mosaic pictures are formed from glass shards reflected in mirrors. In Europe these were sold in the 19th century at village fairs, and they are a favourite toy to this day. They are also known in the Far East.

Dolls whose surface consisted of densely sewn tiny glass beads form a special group of glass toys. They are characteristic of the Sotho, Ovambo, Zulu and other southern African peoples. The craft is still flourishing today, though toys are only one of the items of the South African 'bead culture', which began in the 18th century. Arranged in geometric patterns of contrasting colours, they form a kind of decorative covering for a variety of objects.

189

210 Figure of a Zulu doll consisting of bead bracelets over a fabric base. South Africa, early 1980s. H. 23.5 cm.

Glass beads were a favourite decorative element among North American tribes, and they appear, for instance, on Dakota Indian dolls, though figures made entirely of beads are most likely of more modern vintage. From the Zuñi of New Mexico, we have an authenticated figure of a nun made between 1930 and 1960, the entire surface of which is covered with tightly sewn black and white beads.

Stone toys are not a major category in recent times, but the tradition of stone toys is rich and ancient: they have emerged from numerous archaeological sites. Among the most frequently mentioned ancient toys is the limestone figure of a hedgehog on wheels discovered in the town of Susa in Iran and dating from the 11th century B.C. From ancient Egypt we have limestone genre figures of the 18th Dynasty, and stone dolls of the 12th Dynasty. Stone balls have been known in Europe since the Middle Ages, though they are hardly very popular today. They were usually made of marble, sometimes of agate. Miniature domestic implements, such as a stone spice-grinder from West Bengal, have survived in museum collections in India.

In Bolivia and Peru small stone figures of llamas, horses and miniature dishes were sold for witches' rituals during the Alacitas festival, the holiday of plenty, which falls in January. After the rites were completed, the figures were given to children as playthings. The Mapuche of Chile made small bowls of volcanic lava.

Toys of bone and walrus ivory were carved and used in the most northern territory of the North American continent.

211 Doll in Seminole costume decorated with fancy binding. Florida, U.S.A., 1960s. H. 24 cm.

212 Horse and ibex fashioned from woollen fibres wound round a wooden figure. Addis Ababa, Ethiopia, acquired in 1988. L. horse 21 cm, h. ibex 27 cm.

213 Miniature leather sandals used as both a gift and a toy. Aimar, La Paz, Bolivia, before 1937. L. 6.2 cm.

In Alaska, by the Bering Sea, Eskimo girls played with dolls carved from them by their fathers. To make it easier to dress them, the dolls had upraised hands and sometimes no legs. A special girl's toy was the so-called 'story knife', carved from walrus ivory. The girls drew objects in the snow or the ground based on stories from their own imagination. They kept the story knives until adulthood and very often handed them down to their own daughters.

In Mongolia, goat, sheep and antelope are carved from animal bone, as are dice which have an animal's name on each side. The animal's value reflects its importance in real life. Children also play with the dice in the same way as others play with marbles.

Cloth toys form a very large group, but unfortunately their vulnerability to wear and tear means that few have survived from earlier times. In general they are essentially home-made toys, sometimes

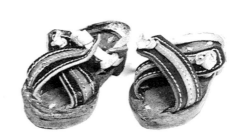

214 Dolls representing
a married couple, either
a king and queen, or
a merchant and his wife,
made of impregnated and
painted fabric stiffened with
paper. Gwalior, Madhya
Pradesh, India, 1980.
H. 14.5 cm, 18.5 cm.

made by the children themselves: historical survivals attain the statues of museum
pieces for their rarity, not for their aes-
thetic value!

The earliest evidence of rag dolls and
dolls' clothes comes from ancient Egypt,
from Roman tombs and from the Arab
world about the 8th century. Suitable climatic conditions prevail there and rag
dolls have survived for the same reason at
the opposite end of the world in South
America. The graves of the Chankai culture in Peru (13th—15th centuries) con-

tained dozens of cloth dolls with painted
and embroidered faces. Besides individual figures, whole genre scenes have survived; for example, a weaver sitting at
a loom and a boat filled with passengers.

The simplest type of rag doll is the
European type with a knotted handker-
chief for a head. Mainly known from 19th-
century literature, today they are known
primarily through reconstructions. In
Central Europe the rag 'infant' (12 to
25 cm long) was produced by professional makers and sold at markets; reports of

194

them occur in the Netherlands, Czechoslovakia, Hungary, Rumania, Russia and Yugoslavia. In 20th-century Europe, all sorts of fabric animals were produced by professional designers who drew on folk traditions or were inspired by Far Eastern rag toys.

Fabric animals in bright colours were turned out in China, the most common being tigers, carp, and dogs. Chinese lanterns in the shape of animals such as dogs or crabs were also produced. In Japan cotton-fabric copies of vegetables and sets of animals with drums and banners are found.

Rag dolls, mostly home-made, are one of the few toys whose existence is documented in the large cultural area of the Near East and North Africa. Individual dolls and whole sets, dating from the end of the 19th and beginning of the 20th century, are known from Libya, Egypt, Syria, Turkey, Iran and Afghanistan.

Among the best-known Indian rag toys are dolls from Bihar, most of which are free-standing with outstretched arms: the face is generally embroidered or painted. Figures of animals such as the rhinoceros and the horse were made in several other Indian states, including Assam and Rajasthan.

A 16th-century drawing by John White shows an American Indian squaw with her daughter, who is holding a cloth doll. European dolls thus appeared among the Algonkin at a very early date. Home-made rag dolls, sewn by American Indian women in the 19th century, usually are dressed in leather garments, sometimes embroidered with glass beads. The children of the colonists played with similar dolls, but these were naturally dressed in European clothes. Besides 'white' rag dolls, black ones — known by the now taboo name *golliwogs* — were very popular with white children.

Modern rag dolls from Latin America are scarce, apparently unknown outside Mexico. In Bolivia and Peru, however, villagers made woollen dolls' clothes in the 19th century, and perhaps they made the dolls as well.

Apart from dolls, infants and animal figures, clothes were sewn or knitted for rag, wood, leather and ceramic dolls. These are to be found all over the world, with the exception of the far north where leather is the fashion.

215 Rag doll, glass buttons, painted face. Navajo, U.S.A., 1930—31. One of a set of dolls sewn for Navajo children. H. 19 cm.

Toy Theatres

The puppet theatre is a world where entertainment for adults and children merge, where the borderline between children's play and adult entertainment can scarcely be distinguished. The fantastic quality and stylization of the puppet world, the result of employing inanimate actors, enthralls adults and children alike.

The overwhelming majority of puppets are made by adult professionals. Only during the 20th century, at least in Europe, does one come across puppets made by children.

Puppets can be divided into three groups according to the way they are manipulated: string puppets, or marionettes; puppets manipulated from below, such as rod puppets and glove and hand puppets; and shadow puppets — manipulated from behind or below and moving only in two-dimensional space.

A special category, related to 'folk' theatre and traditional children's puppet theatre, is the historical or religious tableau. The connection between puppet theatre and religion is strong throughout Asia, Africa and South America; it is somewhat less evident in Europe, though a classic example of it is the Polish *szopki* — Nativity scenes taken around from house to house during the Christmas season. Productions of *szopki* attained their greatest popularity and highest quality in the Cracow area, where the tradition has survived to the present day. Although the custom of arranging Nativity scenes came to Poland from Italy in the 13th century, the *szopki* developed much later, not until after 1700. At that time, when figures and scenes from everyday life featured in the Nativity scenes, moving figures manipulated from behind were introduced for the first time. From the end of the 19th century it appears that *szopki* of several sizes were made in winter by building workers.

Whereas the larger examples served religious purposes, smaller ones were bought as children's gifts. Since the 1950s, *szopki* have been made for use in the puppet theatre.

In the history of the European puppet theatre the most important and oldest role is played by marionettes, or puppets manipulated by strings from above. The earliest accounts of such puppets appear in the works of several Classical authors, including Xenophon in the 4th century B.C. Experts argue, however, whether the ancient puppet theatre outlived the fall of the Roman Empire and whether there was a continuous line of development to the Middle Ages. The oldest medieval representation of marionettes is to be found in a manuscript, *Hortus deliciarum*, which is dated 1160. *Alexandreida*, a Czech epic poem of 1338 about Alexander the Great, appears in an illuminated manuscript, the illustrations of which include a scene of two hand puppets being watched by three children.

Evidence of the existence of the puppet theatre in Europe then multiplies swiftly. During the 16th century specific mention of puppets appears in the records of several German towns and in Bohemia, and at the end of the 16th century the types of puppets found in the folk theatres of the 19th century, such as the English comic-macabre Punch and Judy, or the French Polichinelle and Madame Gigogne, were already in being.

The repertoire of puppet ensembles was probably based on chivalric romances and the *commedia dell'arte* tradition, which persists to the present day in Sicilian puppet theatre. Only at the end of the 18th century at the earliest, were orthodox theatrical dramas adapted for puppet theatres. At the same time historical plays and plays with an educational or nationalistic purpose began to be written specifically for puppet theatre. During the 18th and early 19th centuries other types emerged, notably folk puppet comedies. The German Hanswurst, the Viennese Kasperl and the Czech Kašpárek — probably a combination of Harlequin and Pantaloon, two comic types of the *commedia dell'arte* — were created.

216 Three examples of the 'one-actor theatre':
(A) Perhaps a play about Hercules, in a miniature from the book by Johan de Grice *Romance of Alexander* from the 13th-14th century in England.
(B) Czech glove theatre with Caspar (Kašpárek), the Grim Reaper and the rabbit, 19th century.
(C) Japanese touring theatre, woodcut, 19th century.

From the mid-19th century, the domestic puppet theatre was publicized in educational literature, with instructions on how to build a set and paint the scenery. In the second half of the 19th century, this led to a considerable expansion of puppet theatre, which if not still expanding is more or less stabilized today. Domestic puppet theatres were produced in France, Germany, Britain and other countries.

Glove puppets probably developed at the same time as marionettes, but in Europe this type is somewhat more recent. In fact, theatres for glove or hand puppets are apparently a 19th-century development. It was the custom for touring theatres manned by a single puppeteer to follow travelling fairs or visit towns on occasions of some celebration. He (occasionally she) was sometimes accompanied by a single musician. A news-sheet of the mid-19th century traces the journey of one such little theatre on a troop vessel headed for Sevastopol, from Marseille (France) at the time of the Crimean War, its purpose being to amuse the French soldiers going out to fight. This type of theatre still exists unchanged in certain parts of Italy, including Rome. The core of the repertoire consists of two comedians, three or more comic puppets, sometimes combined with the use of small, live animals such as guinea pigs or rabbits. The puppets often react — usually mockingly — to contemporary conditions or conflicts. They exist in many countries — Russia, Bohemia, Austria, Germany, France and Britain. The glove puppets often reflect the comic types of marionette, such as Kašpárek, Kasperl, Hanswurst, Polichinelle and Mr. Punch. The common ancestor of all of them is the forebear of today's Italian Pulcinella, unless, as some say, they have a common ancestor in the Turkish comic hero, Karagöz.

In south-eastern Europe growth of 'shadow' theatre reflected the expanding frontiers of the Ottoman Empire. Evidence of its existence comes from Bosnia, Herzegovina and Greece, where a comic figure appears in the form of the prankster Karankiores.

It was from there that the shadow theatre spread in the 17th century to southern Italy and later to Northern Europe, especially Germany. Some 17th-century civic records contain requests from profession-

218   Shadow puppets and props, painted leather, 19th century:
(A) Boat with archers. Egypt.
(B) Chest. Sarajevo, Bosnia and Herzegovina.
(C) Night watchman — Turkish puppet.
(D) Soldier — Turkish puppet.
(E) Camel rider. Alepo, Syria. Probably of Turkish origin.
(F) Karagöz. Istanbul, Turkey.

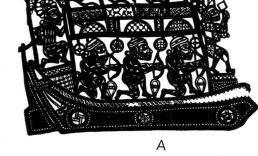

A

B

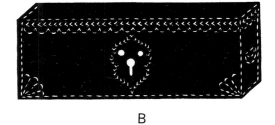

C   D

E   F

◀

217 Puppets from
a 'family' puppet theatre in
Bohemia (from the
left, devil, 'Czech' Johnny,
dwarf, king and princess),
1930s. They date from the
end of the 19th century and
were the work of the popular
Czech painter Mikoláš Aleš,
considered a 'national' artist.
Workshops producing such
puppets went out of business
in the 1950s.
H. *c.* 20 cm.

al actors to be allowed to perform 'Italian shadows' at the marketplace in towns such as Bremen, Frankfurt and Danzig (Gdańsk), but this form of puppet theatre did not make any profound impression on popular culture.

Western Europe probably copied the shadow theatre from the Chinese, which was known in France in 1767. Many instructions were published in the 19th century on how to cut out silhouettes, objects and figures from paper (or other media). The principle of shadow puppets and shadow theatre is still sometimes exploited in the modern, commercial theatre.

Most folk theatres and plays went out of existence in Europe in the wake of the Industrial Revolution. They were revived in some countries such as the former Soviet Union, in connection with state support for folk art, or for nationalist motives, which encouraged developments in Bohemia in

219 Shadow puppet,
goatskin painted with
organic colours. The figure
represents Sita, heroine of
the *Ramayana* epic.
Andhra Prapesh, India, end
of 19th or beginning of 20th
century. H. 120 cm.

the late 19th and early 20th centuries.

In Mediterranean countries, whether in Europe, Asia or Africa, Islamic and Christian cultural values mingled. The Near East provided a model for shadow theatre in south-eastern Europe, although the historical roots of this culture lay farther away, in India and the Far East.

In the Near East, shadow puppets played a decisive role in folk theatre, but other types were used by gypsy puppeteers and touring entertainers.

Ibn Hazim (1211—85), the Moorish scholar, mentions shadow theatre in his book of aphorisms. Another Muslim scholar, Ibn al-Arabi, mentioned this type of theatre, intended for children, in 1231 and praised it highly.

The oldest reference to the Turkish shadow theatre occurs in the same century. It played, under Mongol rule, in cities of Central Asia such as Khodzhent, Tashkent, Khiva, Bukhara and Samarkand. At the beginning of the 17th century the standard characters were already established. The 19th-century traveller Ewliya Chelebi describes in his account of his travels: the jester Karagöz, with his constant changes of clothing, pilgrims to Mecca, soldiers, beggars and other comic figures. He lists a number of popular comedies with titles like *Three Bandits* and *The Arab Beggar and the Soldier.*

The heroes of many Turkish comedies are a two-man team — the clowns or jesters known as Karagöz and Hawacit. According to legend, in the 14th century there were two jesters living in the town of Bursa, then capital of the Ottoman state, who were constantly making fun of the sultan. They were therefore executed, but the sultan missed their jokes so much that he had leather shadow puppets made in their image, and they have continued to this day. Many jokes and anecdotes are ascribed to them, handed down orally from generation to generation, though by now they have all been written down.

The oldest report of puppet theatre in Iran dates from the 12th century, but it is not certain whether it is a description of true marionettes. A clearer indication appears in the work of the Persian poet Nizami (c. 1141 — c. 1209); and there is reliable evidence of shadow theatre in Tabriz in the 14th century.

Shadow puppets were cut from donkey or cattle hide, which was thinned to the point of transparency, then painted and oiled, to maintain the transparent effect. The heroes are normally cut in profile and usually have movable arms and legs. Sometimes they have interchangeable heads. They are manipulated by rods attached to the body and moving parts. During performance the puppets are placed behind a lighted screen so that the audience sees clearly outlined silhouettes. By moving the puppet away from the screen, the clarity of outline is reduced; thus the puppets can be brought into or out of sharp focus as the progress of the plot demands.

The composition of a puppet theatre ensemble differs from region to region, ranging from puppeteer plus musician to quite a large group of handlers, speakers and musicians.

There are three basic types of puppet theatre in India — marionettes, hand-puppets and shadow puppets — but the spread of individual types depended on local historical and cultural traditions. The oldest reports of the existence of a puppet theatre date from c. 200 B.C. and have survived in a Tamil manuscript *Tirukkural,* and also in Sanskrit literature. According to some theories, the puppet theatre was 'invented' in India and spread from there to China and South-east Asia. In India, it is generally considered the oldest type of theatre, because the main figure of classical Hindu drama, the character who introduces and directs the whole performance, is *sutradhara,* 'the one who holds the thread in his hand', i.e. a puppeteer. It seems that a direct line of development can be traced from the shadow-theatre plays of the 13th century to the present repertoire. The productions have retained some religious features, for instance; they are performed during religious holidays and are sometimes part of temple ritual. According to popular belief, a play has magical powers to drive away evil spirits and infectious diseases or to induce rain.

In Rajasthan, marionettes performed in plays drawing on local history and stories from the historical epic, the *Ramayana.* The performance is usually accompanied by a drum. The puppeteer and his assistant also speak for the puppets.

In the Karnataka (Maisur) area both marionettes and shadow theatre are known. The marionettes differ from those

200

220   Marionette, wood with polychrome
decoration and fabric, representing the
heroine of a Rajput historical play. Udaipur,
Rajasthan, India, 1970s. The puppet was
made by a local village carver in the Udaipur
museum. Based on traditional models.
H. 46 cm.

201

221　Marionettes, wood with polychrome
decoration and fabric. Part of a set of
puppets used for children's plays. Mandalay,
Burma, before 1962. H. 19.5 cm and 21 cm.

222   Marionette depicting Buddha's horse
Kandik, wood with polychrome decoration.
Rangoon, Burma, before 1969. The horse is
one of a set of puppets used for adults'
performances. H. 30 cm, l. 23.5 cm.

223   Miniature rod puppets, painted
modelling material. China, before 1956.
They depict the heroes of classical Chinese
drama: the warrior, the actor and the demon.
They are modelled from a mixture of rice
dough and papier mâché. H. 5.3—5.6 cm.

224   Rag glove-puppets in costumes of
different Mexican states (Pueblo,
Chiapas, Veracruz). Mexico, before 1961.
Part of a larger set of souvenir playthings.
H. 49 cm, 41 cm and 50 cm.

225　The Grim Reaper — a rod puppet,
painted plywood, intended for All Saints'
Day festival. Oaxaca region or Mexico City,
Mexico, before 1982. H. 25.5 cm, l. 23 cm.

226 Contemporary
costume doll, wood with
polychrome decoration and
fabric. Japan, 1970s. The
costume is made at home.
Customers buy the wooden
figure whose face and hands
are painted. They depict
a young girl, a housewife
and a geisha. The tradition
of making these 'Isho' dolls
goes back to the 17th
century. H. 25 cm.

207

227   Quechua married couple — souvenir
costume dolls. Bolivia, before 1964. H. 14.5
and 16 cm.

of Rajasthan mainly in the way they are handled: the puppeteer holds them using not only his hands but also his head, on which he wears a ring with strings attached to the heads of the puppets. The puppets' arms and legs are moved by rods. Among the most popular plays is one about the pastoral life of Krishna.

The shadow puppets are the same size as the marionettes. The latter are made in groups, and are usually not articulated, the figures of the main characters having movable hands and legs and a separate head. The figures are richly carved and beautifully painted. Two basic types of plays are known: comedies featuring the prankster Killakyata and his ugly wife Bangarakka, and stories from the *Mahabharata* and *Ramayana* and from Krishna's life. Even the more serious plays are often enlivened by the appearance of Killakyata and Bangarakka.

Performances are given from evening until dawn and continue for several nights in succession. A complete version of the *Ramayana* can last 41 nights; even an abridged version takes a week or two.

There are reports of all three types of puppet theatre co-existing in Orissa. Touring companies in the past performed with all three: wooden and paper marionettes, hand puppets and shadow pup-

228   Chinese shadow puppets, painted leather, 20th century:
(A) Warrior. H. 32 cm.
(B) Young girl. H. 32 cm.
(C) Pedlar. H. 25 cm.
(D) Figure used in acrobatic scenes. H. 30 cm.

pets. Figures of animals such as buffaloes and snakes also featured, and the repertoire included stories about the life of Krishna and parts of the *Ramayana* itself.

From Andhra Pradesh, where only the shadow theatre is known, come the largest Indian puppets, almost life-size. As early as the 16th century, the story of Rama and Sita was adapted for the shadow theatre; the appearance of the puppets was clearly prescribed and adhered to at least until the 19th century, when there was a decline in artistic quality. The size of the puppets is related to their importance in the drama. Besides religious themes, there are also comic appearances of Killakyata and his wife.

In Uttar Pradesh only hand-puppets were used. Favourite productions include the comedy *Gulabo-Sitabo,* based on the names of its two main heroes, the wives of a Muslim who are constantly quarrelling. The puppets have wooden heads and fabric bodies, and the play is accompanied by drum beats. The drummer and the puppeteer provide the puppets' voices.

Immovable shadow puppets were known on the Malabar coast; in Bengal, rod puppets, with interchangable heads, were common.

In South-east Asia there were both marionette and shadow theatres. Shadow puppets from Burma and Thailand are outstanding for their beauty and were painted for day- or night-time performances. The day-time puppets were painted in brighter colours and with greater care for detail. Javanese types, almost one metre high and dressed in gorgeous costumes, were used. The heads were usually made of papier mâché and lacquered; their introduction to Thailand occurred probably in the second half of the 17th century. Shadow puppets were certainly known in Cambodia and Malaysia in 1458, and no doubt earlier. Complete sets comprised about 150 characters and were divided into several categories: princes and princesses, demons, nature spirits, monkey heroes, and others. In the latter category were farmers, ascetics, etc. The costumes drew on those of the actors in the royal ballet.

Only marionettes were used in Burma; those that performed for adults were one metre high, while those playing to children were about 20 cm. The beginnings of the Burmese tradition are placed only in the second half of the 18th century. Apart from people and gods, animals are featured in the cast, and were made either of papier mâché or carved from wood, brightly painted, and sometimes clothed. The subjects drew on stories from the life of Buddha and the adapted versions of the *Ramayana.*

Indonesia also has a very old tradition of shadow theatre, the oldest reliable reference occurring in the 9th or 10th century. In the 11th century, several verses of the poem *The Marriage of Aryunov* were devoted to it. Discussion still continues as to whether the tradition is indigenous or whether it was derived from India. Unlike India, performances in Indonesia were watched from both sides of the illuminated sheet: most of the audience in fact sits behind the puppeteers and musicians. The audience on the other side was formerly women and segregation, though no longer by sex, still exists.

Stories about Rama and Sita, in which they appear in the guise of different animal heroes, are popular in Bali. In Java, stories from the cycle about the royal Pandu family are presented, interspersed with local legends and tales, as well as plays tracing the course of human life. These are usually improvised, although they have a definite subject and are generally in a historical setting.

As in many other fields, China has the oldest puppet-theatre tradition, which is essentially an art of the people. According to oral tradition, written down a thousand years later, the first puppets appeared in the 10th century B.C. at the court of the Emperor Mu-wang of the Chou Dynasty (1122–221 B.C.).

Puppet performances had a common, no doubt religious, origin with the use of masks, the term for both being *giu-li-xi.* Throughout the last millennium, there were frequent references to the puppet theatre in literature.

Chinese puppet theatre embraces many forms. The first, the classic street theatre, is performed in a kind of booth on portable columns, concealing the single performer below the stage. The performer (and proprietor) carries the booth on his shoulders; when a sufficiently large audience has been attracted by his striking a gong, he sets up the construction wherever he happens to be and the performance begins. He uses hand-puppets, the

229 Puppet, stained wood.
Bambara, Mali, 1970s.
Puppets such as these
apppear in plays of a comic
character and perform
especially in the Mopti and
San areas. Besides the
reversible, Janus-like
puppets, puppets with
several heads growing out of
a single neck or from one
shoulder are found.
H. 34.5 cm, w. 7.5 cm.

211

ensemble usually consisting of 36 characters, which have the physical proportions of adults, i.e. small heads in relation to the body. The puppet's limbs and head are of painted wood and the head has a movable mouth. Favourite subjects are drawn from legends about the journey to India of the monk Tripitaka and his animal guides.

Other types of puppet theatre required a more stable construction. The beginnings of the marionette theatre are linked to the rule of the Emperor Gao-Zu of the Han Dynasty (206-194 B.C.). Other companies used rod puppets, manipulated from behind by horizontally held rods. The puppets are usually very realistic and appear in historical plays, detective stories and legends. In the 19th century, the main centre of this type of folk theatre was Shantung province. In seasons when there was little agricultural work, puppetry adepts learned from more experienced performers the art of manipulating puppets and memorised the texts of plays. This training period lasted three winters; only after that could the apprentice begin his own career. Puppeteers travelled not only across China but also to Korea and Japan, though by the 19th century, many of them were concentrated around Peking. In Shantung province every year there were festivals with hundreds of puppeteers taking part, but puppets and theatre companies existed in all the provinces.

The beginning of shadow-theatre history is connected with the Emperor Wu-ti, of the Han Dynasty, who lived c. 120 B.C. According to legend, when his favourite wife died the royal seer brought her image back to life using shadow puppets.

During the Sung Dynasty (A.D. 960 to 1279) the popularity of the shadow theatre increased throughout China and became an authentic people's theatre; it was revived again under the Ming Dynasty (1368-1643), the first mention of leather puppets being from this period; in the earlier Sung period they were made of paper. The popularity of the shadow theatre continued under the Manchu rulers and is undimmed to this day.

Two artistic traditions are evident in both the types of shadow puppets and the repertoire. The so-called shadow plays of Lan-chou, also known as eastern shadow plays or, rather confusingly, the northern school, form one tradition. The puppets are transparent, relatively small and very brightly painted. The basic repertoire included written plays based on historical stories or literary adaptations of fairytales. In the 19th century this school acquired great popularity in Peking, where the tradition of an established theatre company began. Such a theatre consists of about eight people: one or two manipulate the puppets; two speak the voices and four play the music. In the western shadow-puppet theatre (or southern school), which dates back to the Sung period, the puppets are usually cut from leather; they are larger and less brightly painted. The plays are folk stories, fairy tales and histories that have been passed on orally. The emphasis is on improvisation, the origins of this school dating from the Sung Dynasty.

Historical records confirm that other types of puppet theatres existed. They included the 'powder' theatre, whose puppets, it has been suggested, were moved by exploding gunpowder, and the live 'puppet' theatre in which child actors imitated the movements of puppets. These children's performances were given in the Sung period, at least 700 years earlier than the European equivalent. The 'floating' theatre consisted of wooden puppets drawn by bamboo or wires on the surface of ponds, lakes or pools. It has persisted from the 12th century to the 20th in Vietnam, where scenes from the life of villagers and the aristocracy, dramatized stories and tales of mythical animals are performed.

Although we are sometimes unable to imagine just how certain types of Chinese theatre looked, it is clear that all these varieties were open to the public and therefore intended for the broadest audience. The development of theatre was linked to the development of cities and professional entertainment generally; most performances were given in marketplaces or on the streets. From the 17th century, there are references to family-owned marionette theatres in which children manipulated the puppets. A scene from such a children's performance is shown on a 17th-century scroll called 'One Hundred Children', but this was an event for wealthier audiences.

In Japan the puppet theatre also has a long tradition, the earliest reference being from the 9th century A.D. It mentions puppeteers (not defined more precisely) who carried box theatres hung from their necks in which they enacted stories about the foundation of famous shrines. The oldest actual descriptions of the puppets come from the 11th–13th centuries, the documents having survived in the treasuries of shrines and temples. To judge from these descriptions, the rod puppet was used. In the 14th century, the Japanese imported marionettes, but they did not prove a great success. Only in the 17th century, with a more integrated performance incorporating greater co-operation between the actor-puppeteer and the musician, were the foundations laid for the renowned type of Japanese theatre known as *bunraku*; this theatre, however, is an urban phenomenon and is played before an adult audience.

In Tokushima prefecture, puppeteers travelled through villages with rod puppets. During a performance one man manipulated the puppets and spoke for them, while his two colleagues provided the music. The same type of puppets were used on Sado Island, where the entire performance was the work of a single puppeteer. The repertoire included, besides historical plays, licentious comedies whose roots go back to the 17th century.

In many parts of Japan, marionettes are used in traditional plays, such as *The Lions' Dance;* performances on Awaji Island can also be considered part of the

people's theatre. These puppeteers perform in schools and public halls. Their puppets and manner of presentation come from the *bunraku* theatre; the only difference is the subject of the plays.

The Japanese hand-puppet theatre also expanded after 1868, and to this day in the Gumma prefecture touring puppeteers perform not only in theatres but also in the street.

The shadow theatre in Japan is associated with Osaka, but there are several other types, like the theatre in Hachioji, near Tokyo, differing according to the method by which the puppets are manipulated.

North Africa was for centuries part of the Mediterranean cultural area, and it is no surprise that the same type of shadow theatre found in the Near East and Turkey is also characteristic of Tunisia, Algeria and Egypt, which were part of the Turkish empire for many centuries. By the 14th century, Egyptian writers were producing plays for the shadow theatre: three plays by Ibn Daniyal, who died in 1311, have survived. The shadow theatre was still performed in Egypt and Tunisia at the beginning of the 20th century. Egyptian plays were based mainly on traditional historical subjects, such as the wars against the Persians or the Nubians.

Sub-Saharan Africa falls into a different category. Rod puppets and hand-puppets manipulated from below or from the back were characteristic. In all surviving examples, the puppets, or at least their heads and bodies, are carved from wood; sometimes they are painted.

From the territory of northern Nigeria and the area around Lake Chad there are reports from the beginning of the 20th century of theatrical performances of a comic character. The main protagonists are two rascals, the subject of local folktales, who try to trick everyone and each other as well. The cast is completed by a judge, a pilgrim returning from Mecca and some girls hunting for husbands. The plays were performed with hand-puppets over a simple screen, behind which the performer was hidden. During the performance, the actor was accompanied by four musicians. The origins of these plays and the puppets themselves are obscure; the puppeteers' own tradition suggests they originated among the Kanuri of modern Nigeria and Chad.

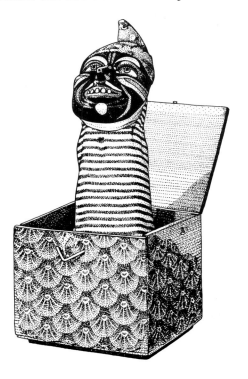

230 Movable toy — out of the box jumps Mr Punch, a favourite hero of the English folk theatre. U.S.A., 19th century.

213

In pre-colonial times there were two types of plays among the Ibibio of Nigeria with wooden rod puppets. The first related to religious occasions, the second had a satirical character. Beggars and various rural characters appeared as comic figures. The actors based their performances on well-known folklore subjects, but also improvised. Besides criticizing local personalities, certain scenes caricatured the behaviour of foreigners, especially Muslims and Europeans. Inter-village strife was a frequent subject. The carved wooden puppets were brightly painted, and some had movable limbs — even a movable head and lower jaw. In the 19th century it seemed as though every large rural community had its own theatre company.

Puppet companies existed also among the Bambara and smaller ethnic groups like the Marka and Bozo, now in Mali. The rod puppets appeared in performances which were sometimes of a religious character and sometimes pure entertainment (often satirical). The behaviour of villagers, gossips, foreigners and anyone outside the community was the frequent subject of satire. The performances were traditionally the responsibility of the village council, which organized local entertainments, and were performed by 14- and 15-year-olds. The puppets, mostly just heads or busts, were carved from wood and stained brown, and sometimes painted. Occasionally the full figures of puppets dressed in fine clothes, for instance, horseback riders, also made an appearance. The area in which this type of performance was staged was probably quite large, since we hear of them in Upper Volta (Burkina Fasso) and northern Ghana. It appears that similar puppets were employed in other activities, which remain mysterious.

The roots of the hugely popular folk theatre in Latin America are European, but they have been thematically adapted to local cultural-historical traditions. Besides pairs of (usually) hand-puppets, plays with larger numbers of 'inanimate actors' were also performed. The subjects for the puppet and the live theatre were often the same. For instance, in Mexico the puppet production of Don Juan is played at All Souls', at the same time as it is performed by actors. The rod puppets represented Death the Reaper and were normally painted in brilliant colours.

In Argentina and Brazil, hand-puppet shows were also popular. Their producers staged plays based on fairy tales such as 'The Death of the Godmother' and 'Concerning the Stupid Devil and the Villagers' or shorter comic scenes, with pairs of puppets. Except for the comic scenes, the same repertoire was performed by actors of touring companies.

The heroes of the children's theatre world are not only performing puppets but also toys. In India a favourite wooden figure, Vidushi, is a comic hero from the puppet theatre, and in Europe the Caspars, Pulcinellas, Petrushkas, etc. were also produced simply as toys.

Souvenirs

Having discussed folk toys of the last two centuries, something must also be said about the similar articles which, increasingly during that period, were sold to tourists as souvenirs. They represent the last stage of development — actually the end — of folk art.

Among the best known and most popular souvenirs of this type are dolls in costume. Their popularity began as early as the 18th century, according to M. Bachmann in his book *Das grosse Puppenbuch*. An example he quotes from that time are 200-year-old straw figures of Venetians in carnival dress. Very realistic figures of pedlars, hawkers and their wares were on sale in England in the 1780s. The dolls which occupied the rooms of early dolls' houses were dressed with meticulous concern for realism; their clothing faithfully reproduced the contemporary garments of country people, city-dwellers and the aristocracy. Other sources of the popularity of costumed dolls may be looked for in the rationalist spirit of the 18th-century Enlightenment and the effects of colonial expansion. One aspect of the Enlightenment encouraged popular interest in the lives of ordinary people, not previously considered worthy of study, and of their culture. Colonial expansion and voyages of exploration heightened popular interest in distant people and places, creating a market for souvenirs. Most frequently these were miniatures of manufactured objects, such as models of boats, but dolls also figured among travellers' mementoes of exotic places. During the 19th century demand continued to grow, and some colonial rulers supported the production of souvenirs. For example, in India the development of souvenir production helped to provide a living for local craftsmen deprived of work by the import of cheap industrial goods. The national colonial exhibitions and provincial industrial exhibitions organized throughout the 19th century helped to publicise the business, and sometimes revived production, of items that had ceased to be made.

The growth of nationalism and the establishment of modern European nations influenced the development of folk souvenirs in Europe. National traditions were studied, 'pure' national culture was sought and researchers of the day, as well as politicians, found the answer in folk culture. A desire to retain and maintain those traditions led to much learned publication — and to attempts to make use of traditional peasant articles as decorative additions to sophisticated city living rooms. To adopt folk costumes would have been going too far, but costume dolls had wide appeal. Studiously authentic costumes were made from the early 19th century though efforts to reproduce the national costume of unfamiliar peoples led to a few curiosities.

Costume dolls were made largely by country women for urban markets, but frequently by urban residents as well, especially, perhaps, those steeped in the nationalist spirit of the time. The dolls also went to museums, educational institutes and other cultural organizations. Even buying such dolls was, in a small way, a patriotic act.

Costume dolls, representing pairs of boys and girls or married couples, are found in all Europe. Figures from the 1860s to the 1880s document the existence of a wide range of types, although the emphasis was usually on especially attractive costumes, such as that of Scottish Highlanders, Basques and Catalans, Bosnians and Heligolanders.

In North America and Africa, dolls inevitably depicted the original, currently

231 Doll made of wood, fabric and wax, wearing costume jewellery. Sudan, before 1911. Its dress, jewels and hairstyle resemble women's costumes of central Sudan. H. 42.7 cm.

▶
232 Baby doll in a papoose and an American Indian, fabric and plaster. U.S.A., end of 19th century. H. 32 cm and 33.5 cm.

second-class, inhabitants. In the United States they were usually Amerindians, including infants in papooses. Pioneer figures — fur-trappers and Indian-fighters — and women in long dresses were also made, often of scraps of cloth and leather. In South Africa in the 1880s Boer children played with leather dolls depicting Xhosa and others, and these also found their way to Europe.

Realistic figures were made in India, where the number of ethnic groups, castes and sub-castes into which the population was divided provided a great many different types.

In China the production of costume dolls did not develop to such a degree, but during the 19th century there was a huge increase in the number of realistic toys modelled from plaster and other sub-

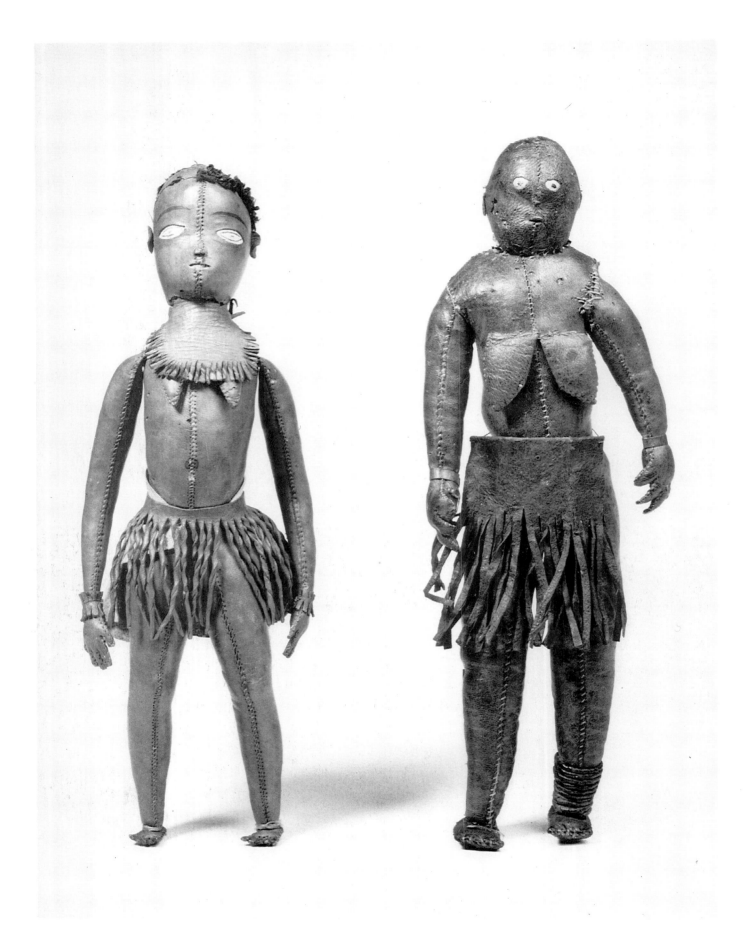

233 Dolls depicting
a Bushman and a Bantu
woman, coloured leather.
Afrikaner, South Africa,
before 1880. Made similarly
to European models, these
were intended for Boer
children. H. 29 cm and 31 cm.

234   Figure of an American
Indian, wood decorated with
a burned pattern and
feather. Xingu River basin,
Brazil, 1970s. H. 22 cm.

235   Models of Alpine
houses obtained in *c.* 1930.
H. 3 cm, l. 6.5 cm.

236   Village house, wood with polychrome decoration. Jedlina village, Bohemia, 1925. The production of wooden toys was introduced by the local teacher after 1918 to help families improve their financial situation. The models were based on the buildings in Jedlina and environs: the inn, chapel, parish house, belfry, etc. H. 6.5 cm.

237   (A, B) Set of furniture with box, wood with polychrome decoration, painted. Bohemia, 1920s. A modern toy-puzzle based on folk models. H. chair 11.8 cm, table 7 cm, dimensions of furniture block 7 × 13 × 6 cm.

A

stances suitable for moulding, which drew on an older tradition. Realistic figures of people and animals were the work of specialized masters, valued for their precise craftsmanship and the skill shown in miniaturization of intricate detail.

In Japan the production of costume dolls drew on the old traditions of children's holidays — the Girls' Festival on March 3 and the Boys' Festival on May 5. The main centres of production were Edo (Tokyo) and Kyoto. The form of these dolls or puppets was established during the 19th century and dominated by the style of Edo. They represented royal couples, courtiers, musicians and others. Some, as early as the 18th century, were dressed in royal clothing of the Heian Dynasty (A.D. 794—1135). Today, dolls are still made depicting heroines of historical plays or stories, or of figures in famous love stories. For boys there are figures of warriors, both mythical and historical, famous heroes, etc. A favourite figure is, naturally, the samurai. Some samurai fig-ures are dressed in medieval clothing or armour.

The production of costume souvenir dolls has continued throughout the 20th century. It has become very widespread (for instance) in Latin America, where dolls are knitted from wool or sewn cotton fabric, especially in the Andean region. Simple figures are made by the inhabitants of the Amazon rain forest and the Orinoco basin.

Since the end of the 19th century, costume dolls from both North and South America have progressed towards realism, in the dolls themselves as human figures more than in their costumes. While, at the end of the 19th century, the carving and modelling of dolls had become rather rigidly stylised, the introduction of new materials has made them more realistic. Evidence of this can be seen in the production of Seminole Indian figures from Florida, models of Eskimo in kayaks, and the crews of whaling boats from British Columbia among others.

B

238 Wooden constructional plaything known as *to-tak*. Zagreb, Croatia, 1966.

Turned wooden figures with painted national, ethnic, or local costumes made their appearance after the Second World War. Judging from their size (about 10 cm), they were intended to be easily portable souvenirs.

Miniature houses — models of Alpine houses, spinning wheels, farming implements and furniture — also fall within the category of souvenir toys. They are found also in many non-European countries, where a frequent subject is a model of the local means of transportation, as well as genre scenes of working craftsmen: a weaver at a loom, a smith at the anvil or a cobbler at his bench, etc. It is sometimes difficult to decide whether they were made merely as souvenir toys or for more serious purposes.

As folk and ethnic art gradually disappears, attempts are made to revive and maintain it. Folk toymaking has the advantage that its products — by virtue of their simplicity, artistic beauty and educational usefulness — are constant favourites.

In European countries, it was mainly ethnographers who became committed to protecting folk toymaking. For example German specialists like O. Seyffert, H. Kluge and T. A. Winde were active in this endeavour in Dresden and Münster during the first half of the 20th century. They strongly influenced a number of Erzgebirge toymakers. To some extent, artists have also helped to maintain the folk toymaking tradition. In Bohemia, efforts to draw on the roots of folk toymaking go back to around 1990, when artists grouped around the Hořice toymaking co-operative, and later the Artěl co-operative, became interested in the subject. Since 1945, as a result of their efforts, an organization called Central Folk Art Products has taken the lead in the production of toys reconstructed on the basis of ethnographic research.

Similar endeavours exist in other European countries. In modern Danish toymaking, Kay Bojesen, who has himself designed toys, is a well-known name. In some places the making of traditional toys is linked to museums. In the Seiffen outdoor museum in Germany workshops produce classic turned and carved figures and little houses. Some museums in Germany and Czechoslovakia produce, if only occasionally, traditional folk toys. Individual workshops of folk toymakers are supported by the state and in Japan they bask in the glory of the name 'Living National Treasure'.

Designers of toys and artists throughout the world are returning to the simplicity of folk toys, at least in their external appearance. An example is the wooden building set known as *to-tak*, designed by Ante Jakič of Zagreb. Using only 14 wooden elements, it is possible to assemble several dozen animals. Original 'folk' building sets, figures of animals and people, and a variety of wagons and carts still appear. Folk and ethnic toymaking will probably long continue to be an inspiring source of ideas for the modern toymaking industry.

Museums and Institutions with Collections of Folk and Ethnic Toys

For those interested in folk and ethnic toys there are many museums with general collections of folk art as well as special exhibitions devoted to children's toys. Some museums also have displays specially designed for children in which many toys can be found. About 180 museums in the world list toys in their collections; in fact they can probably be found in the collections and depositories of virtually every large general museum. Some of the best known museums of toys and puppets are mentioned below.

Czechoslovakia

Chrudim: Loutkářské muzeum, Mydlářův dům (Soap-maker's House).
   Puppet museum with a collection of European toys; established in 1969.
Egypt
Alexandria: Palace Ras el-Tin.
   Museum of costume dolls; established in 1956.
France
Lyon: Musée de Gadagne (Musée historique de Lyon et Musée international de la marionette), 10 rue de Gadagne.
   Special permanent exhibition of French and world theatre puppets.
Germany
Arnstadt: Schlossmuseum, Schlossplatz 1.
   Collection of historical 18th-century dolls and doll's houses (from 1700 to 1751); established in 1919.
Dresden: Staatliche Puppentheatersammlung, Redebeul, Barkengasse 6.
   Puppet museum, established in 1959.
Grefrath bei Krefeld: Niederrheinsches Freilichtmuseum.
   Toy museum, established in 1973.
Kulmbach: Deutsches Zinnfigurenmuseum, Plassenburg.
   Museum devoted to tin soldiers and tin toys; established in 1929.
Munich: Puppentheatersammlung, St. Jakobs-Platz 1.
   Puppet exposition in the museum.
   Spielzeugmuseum, Alt Rathausturm, Marienplatz.

Toy museum, established in 1983.
Neustadt bei Coburg: Deutsches Trachtenpuppenmuseum, Hindenburgplatz.
   Museum of toys and costume dolls; established in 1929.
Nuremberg: Spielzeugmuseum, Karlstrasse 13. Museum documenting development of toys from the Middle Ages to the present; established in 1966.
Seiffen: Erzgebirgisches Spielzeugmuseum, Ernst Thälmann Strasse 73
   Toy museum; an outdoor museum is part of it. It has a lathe-turning workshop producing Erzgebirge toys; established in 1953.
Sonneberg: Deutsches Spielzeugmuseum. Beethoven Strasse 10.
   Toy museum, established in 1901.
Great Britain
Brighton: Rottingdean Grange, Art Gallery and Museum and National Toy Museum. Established in 1955.
Edinburgh: Museum of Childhood, Hyndford's Close, 38 High Street.
   Museum devoted to children and toys; established in 1955.
London: Bethnal Green Museum, Cambridge Heath Road, E2.
   History museum, collections of dolls and toys; established in 1872.
   Horniman Museum, London Road, Forest Hill, SE 23.
   Collection of Javanese puppets; established in 1890.
   Pollock's Toy Museum, 1 Scala Street.
Warwick: Warwick Doll Museum, Oken's House, Castle Street, WI.
   Established in 1955.
Windsor: Queen Mary's Doll's House, Windsor Castle.
   Spectacular doll's house presented to Queen Mary in the 1920s.
Hungary
Kecskemét: Szórakaténusz. Museum of urban and rural toys (about 1,500 items); established in 1981.
India
Bhawanagar: Children's Museum, Gandhi Smriti.

Museum devoted to children and toys.

New Delhi: International Dolls Museum, Nehru House, Bahadurshah Zafar Marg. Museum of costume dolls from the whole world; established in 1965.

National Children's Museum, Bal Bhavan, Kotla Road.

Museum devoted to children and toys.

Russia

Moscow: Gosudarstvenny kukol'ny muzei imeni Obraztsova, Sadovo Samotechnaya ulitsa 3. Puppet museum, established in 1937.

Zagorsk: Muzei igrushki.

Toy museum, established in 1918.

Switzerland

Riehen: Wettsteinhaus Riehen Spielzeugmuseum.

Toy museum near Basle, established in the 1970s.

United States

New Britain (Conn.): New Britain Children's Museum, 28 High Street.

Toy museum, established in 1957.

Philadelphia (Pennsylvania): Perelman Antique Toy Museum, 270 South 2nd Street. Toy museum, established in 1962. It contains, primarily, factory-made metal toys but also includes a number of wooden and folk tyos.

Saint Augustine (Florida): The Museum of Yesterday's Toys.

Watkins Glen (New York): American Life Foundation and Study Institute, Old Irelandville.

Toy museum, established in 1958.

Select Bibliography

Anonymous, *Illustrated London News*, Dec. 28, 1935

Anonymous, *Museo dell'Uomo* III, No. 103, Milan, 1964

Anonymous, *Kunst als Spiel, Spiel als Kunst, Kunst zum Spiel* (Exhibition catalogue), Recklinghausen, 1969

Anonymous, *Ruská lidová řezba a malba na dřevě 17.-20. století* (Russian folk carving and painting on wood, 17th-20th centuries; Exhibition catalogue), Prague, 1979

Anonymous, *Welt der Kleinen* (Exhibition catalogue), Linz, 1982

Bachmann, M., 'Zur Entwicklung der Erzgebirgischen Holzschnitzerei', *Abhandlungen und Berichte des Staatlichen Museums für Völkerkunde Dresden*, Vol. 22, 1963, pp. 143-156

Bachmann, M., *Das Waldkirchener Spielzeug Musterbuch um 1850*, Leipzig, 1977

Bachmann, M., *Das Sonneberger Spielzeug Musterbuch von 1831*, Leipzig, 1979

Bachmann, M. — Hausmann, C., *Das Grosse Puppenbuch*, Leipzig, 1971

Barenholtz, B. — McClintock, I., *American Antique Toys 1830-1900*, New York, 1980

Bilz, H., *Das Reifendreherhandwerk im Spielwarengebiet Seiffen* (Exhibition catalogue), Seiffen, 1976

Bilz, H., *Museumsführer. Erzgebirgisches Spielzeugmuseum Kurort Seiffen* (Exhibition catalogue), Seiffen, 1983

Boguslavskaya, I., *Russkaya glinyanaya igrushka* (Russian clay toys), Leningrad, 1975

Burian, V., 'K typologii a datování lidové keramické plastiky — koníčka' (On the typology and dating of folk ceramic sculpture — horse), *Čs. etnografie* X, No. 3, 1962, pp. 301-307

Caiger, G., *Dolls in Display. Japan in Miniature*, Tokyo, 1933

Clerq de, F. S. A. — Schmeltz, J. D. E., *Ethnographische Beschrijving von de Westen Noordkunst van Nederlandsch Nieuw-Guine*, Leiden, 1893

Collective, *Das Kind und seine Welt* (Exhibition catalogue), Vienna, 1959

Collective, *State Museum of Ethnography under the Ukrainian SSR Academy of Sciences*, Kiev, 1932

Coq, A., *Volkskundliches aus Ost-Turkestan*, Berlin, 1916

Coretelli, N., *Russkaya krestyanskaya igrushka* (Russian peasant toys), Moscow, 1933

Daiken, L., *Children's Toys throughout the Ages*, London, 1965

Dayrell, E., 'Notes on "Nyam Tunerre" or Cat's Cradle', *Man* XII, No. 87, 1912

Dockstader, F. L., *L'Art Indien de l'Amérique Centrale*, Neuchâtel, 1965

Fraser, A., *A History of Toys*, London, 1966

Fritzsch, K. E. — Bachmann, M., *Deutsches Spielzeug*, Leipzig, 1977

Gantskaya, O. A., *Narodnoe iskusstvo Pol'shi* (Folk art of Poland), Moscow, 1970

Garstang, J., 'Excavations at Beni-Hasan', *Man* III, No. 74, 1903

Gray, J., 'Some Scottish String Figures', *Man* III, No. 66, 1903

225

Gröber, K. — Metzger, J., *Kinderspielzeug aus alter Zeit*, Hamburg, 1965

Harding, J. R., ' "Mwali" Dolls of the Wasaramo', *Man* LXI, No. 83, 1961

Harvey, M., *Crafts of Mexico*, London, 1973

Hercík, E., *Československé lidové hračky* (Czechoslovak folk toys), Prague, 1951

Hilská, V., *Japonské divadlo* (Japanese theatre), Prague, 1947

Hodge, F. W. (ed.), *Handbook of American Indians North of Mexico*, New York, 1959

Jacob, G., *Geschichte des Schattentheaters im Morgen- und Abendland*, Hanover, 1925

Johnová, H., 'Lidové hračky' (Folk toys), *Umění a řemesla*, No. 5, 1965, pp. 184-189

Junod, H. A., *The Life of the South African Tribe*, New York, 1962

Just, J. — Karpinski, J., *Sächsische Volkskunst*, Leipzig, 1982

Kaplan, N., *In the Land of the Reindeer*, Leningrad, 1974

Koch, G. *Materielle Kultur der Gilbert-Inseln*, Berlin, 1961

Koch, G., *Materielle Kultur der Ellice-Inseln*, Berlin, 1965

Krämer, A., *Truk*, Hamburg, 1932

Leith-Ross, S., *Nigerian Pottery*, London, 1970

Lipman, J. — Winchester, A., *Die Volkskunst in America*, Munich, 1974

Lutz, F. E., 'String Figures from the Patomana Indians of British Guiana', *Anthropological Papers of the American Museum of Natural History* XII, Part 1, 1912, pp. 1-14

Maas, A., 'Durch Zentral-Sumatra', *Zeitschrift für Ethnologie* 41, 1909, pp. 143 to 166

Malý, L., *Hračky dětí československých* (Toys of Czechoslovak children), Prague, 1895

Mandel, J. J. — Brenier-Estrine, A., 'Clay Toys of Mopti', *African Arts* X, No. 2, 1977, pp. 10-13

McCarthy, F. D., *Australian Aboriginal Decorative Art*, Sydney, 1962

Melniková-Papoušková, N., *Lidové hračky* (Folk toys), Prague, 1948

Michalides, P., *Ľudové hračky na Slovensku* (Folk toys in Slovakia), Bratislava, 1972

Mookerjee, A., *Indian Dolls and Toys*, New Delhi, 1968

Nixdorf, H., *Tönender Ton* (Exhibition catalogue), Berlin, 1974

Pal, M. K., *Catalogue of Folk Art in the Asuntosh Museum*, Calcutta, 1962

Passarge, S., *Adamawa*, Berlin, 1895

Petrie, F., *Objects of Daily Use*, London, 1927

Přibíková, H., 'Cínoví vojáčci a ti druzí' (Tin soldiers and the others), *Umění a řemesla*, No. 4, 1976, pp. 36-46

Ratzel, F., *Völkerkunde*, Vol. III, Leipzig, 1888

Roh, J., *Altes Spielzeug*, Munich, 1958

Schmolitzky, O., *Volkskunst in Thüringen vom 16. bis zum 19. Jahrhundert*, Weimar, 1958

Segy, L., *African Sculpture Speaks*, New York, 1975

Sigrid, P., 'Afrikanische Fantasteinspiele', *Zeitschrift für Ethnologie* 96, 1971, pp. 32 to 70

Sloane, E., *ABC Book of Early Americans*, New York, 1963

Spielenwaren-Anzeiger (Magazine published between 1926 and 1935 in Planá near Mariánské Lázně, Bohemia)

Steward, J. H. (ed.), *Handbook of South American Indians*, New York, 1963

Talbot, P. A., *Life in Southern Nigeria*, London, 1923

Tatsuo, M., *Happy Origami — Whale Book*, Tokyo, 1960

Whitton, B., *Toys. The Knopf Collector's Guide to American Antiques*, New York, 1984

Zíbrt, Č., 'České divadlo loutkové' (Czech puppet theatre), *Český lid* XIX, 1906, pp. 35-50

List of Illustrations

Unless otherwise indicated, the illustrations are from the collection of the Náprstek Museum in Prague.

1 (A) Fragments of women's figures and a bull, ceramic. Culture of the Indus River basin, 2500-1500 B.C. (Náprstek Museum Photo Archives).
(B) Dolls, wood. Egypt. The first is from the Roman period, the other two from the period of the 12th-18th Dynasties (according to Petrie 1927, tab. LI, 380 and 385, tab. LV, 600).

2 Doll, figure made of calabash, twine and putty, with glass beads. Ngwato, Zimbabwe, before 1880.

3 Jointed dolls. The first two, ceramic, from Greece, the third, of wood, from the Roman empire, 3rd and 2nd centuries B.C. Musée du Louvre, Paris (according to Bachmann-Hausmann, 1971, Abb. 46, 47).

4 Noah's Ark, polychrome wood. Exported from Europe to Massachusetts, U.S.A., c. 1800. Essex Inst. Salem (according to Fraser, 1966, at 96).

5 Details of a racing game, print on paper and tin painted figures. Bohemia, end of 19th century. Private collection.

6 Doll, stained wood. Ashanti, Ghana, 1960s. Private collection.

7 Miniature sickles, wood and sheet metal. La Paz, Bolivia, 1910.

8 Doll, bone and fabric. Pilagá, Argentina, before 1904.

9 Cow, wood. Brdy area, Bohemia, early 20th century. Museum of Decorative Arts, Prague (according to Hercík, 1951, Pl. C).

10 (A) Dolls, ceramic, painted after drying. Hausa from the town of Anka and Kebbaw from Argungu, Nigeria, mid-20th century. Nigerian Museum, Jos. (according to Leith-Ross, 1970, 34-35).
(B) Figures and objects, unfired clay. Bozo tribe, town of Mopti, Mali, mid-20th century (according to Mandel-Brenier, 1977, 10-13).
(C) Dishes, unfired clay. Fulbe, Saré Doundou village, Senegal, 1969.

11 (A) 'Buzzing wolf' (whip top). Qara Chodzha, eastern Turkestan, China. Museum für Völkerkunde, Berlin (according to Coq, 1916, 13 and Fig. 12).
(B) Spinning top made from a shell. Garua, Nigeria (according to Passarge, 1895, 226).
(C) Spinning top, wood with polychrome decoration. Mexico, before 1982.
(D) Spinning top, wood. Swahili, Tanzania, 1960s.

12 (A) Balls, fabric overlaid with painted reeds, originally used as a rattle. Egypt, 2nd millennium B.C. British Museum, London (according to Fraser, 1966, Fig. 24).
(B) Balls, plaited from strips and pandan screw pine palms. Ellice Islands, western Polynesia, 20th century (according to Koch, 1961, 158, Abb. 104a).
(C) Ball, silk and cotton. Eastern Turkestan, China, beginning of 20th century. Museum für Völkerkunde, Berlin (according to Coq, 1916, 16).

13 Cart and draught animals, bone. South African Republic, mid 20th century (according to Anonymous, 1982, 1).

14 (A) Kites, palm leaves. Ellice Islands, western Polynesia, mid 20th century (according to Koch, 1961, 150, Abb. 102).
(B) Pinwheels, wood with polychrome decoration. Wadimu region, Papua-New Guinea, early 20th century (according to Clerq-Schmeltz, 1893, Pl. 36/11).
(C) Pinwheels, coconut palm leaves. Ninutao and Nukufatau Islands of the Ellice Islands, western Polynesia, 20th century (according to Koch, 1961, 148, Abb. 99).

15 (A) Doll, plaited bast. Brazil, 20th century. Museum für Völkerkunde, Leipzig (according to Bachmann-Hausmann, 1971, Fig. 34).

(B) Doll, palm stalk. Canello, Brazil, 20th century. Museum für Völkerkunde Leipzig (according to Bachmann-Hausmann, 1971, Fig. 7).

(C) Doll, natural asphalt and bark. Karazha, Brazil, 20th century. Museum für Völkerkunde, Leipzig (according to Bachmann-Hausmann, 1971, Fig. 27).

(D) Doll, calabash and natural asphalt. Karazha, Brazil, 20th century. Museum für Völkerkunde, Leipzig (according to Bachmann-Hausmann, 1971, Fig. 19).

16   Figure of giraffe, pine cones and twigs. Central Bohemia, 1980s. Private collection.

17   Pistol and crossbow, wood. Probably Skašov, Bohemia, 20th century (according to Hercík, 1951, 52, Pl. CIV).

18   Sledge, wood. Eskimo, Pangmirtung locality, Baffin Island, Canada, before 1984.

19   (A) Dagger, stained wood. Kubas, Zaire, before 1949.

(B) Small sword, wood and plastic. Mexico, before 1982.

(C) Sword, wood with polychrome decoration. China, before 1956.

(D) Small sword, wood, fabric and tin foil. Nubia, Egypt, 1960s.

20   Radio model, dried and painted clay. Nag Mansour Kuleig, Nubia, Egypt, 1960s.

21   Figures of camels, goat's jawbone, wood and leather. Hilla Duda village, Berti, Sudan, 1965.

22   (A) Kite. Germany, c. 1405. Göttingen University Library (according to Fraser, 1966, Fig. 81).

(B) Carp, coloured and painted paper. Japan, before 1925.

(C) Kite, palm leaf. Ellice Islands, Western Polynesia (according to Koch, 1961, 149, Abb. 100).

(D) Kite, painted paper. Bohemia, 1960s. Private collection.

(E) Kite, painted paper. India, 1920s (according to Náprstek Museum Photo Archives).

23   Folding paper toys.
(A, C) Japan, 20th century (according to Tatsuo, 1960, 2, 7).
(B, D) Bohemia, 19th century (according to Malý, 1895, 69-76).

24   Dolls, printed and painted paper. Japan, before 1925.

25   Bows and arrows,
(A) wood with polychrome decoration. Nevada, U.S.A., before 1889.

(B) wood. Qara Chodzha, eastern Turkestan, China, beginning of 20th century. Museum für Völkerkunde Berlin (according to Coq, 1916, 12).

(C) wood. Mexico, before 1982.

(D) wood. American Indians of U.S. Southwest, 1930-31.

26   Camel and rider, carved from hide. Niloti, southern Sudan, before 1939.

27   Hippopotamus (?), burned wood decoration. Pygmy Epulu, Zaire, c. 1947.

28   Doll, ceramic, of painted clay, fabric clothes. Mohave, U.S.A., before 1914.

29   Sealskin ball decorated with leather appliqué. Chukchi, Siberia, before 1911.

30   Tiered podium with figures depicting the Japanese royal court, wooden slats with polychrome decoration. Japan, before 1925.

31   *Kachina*, wood with polychrome decoration. Hopi, U.S.A., 1920s.

32   Devil in the shape of a tinker, plaster and fabric. Prague, Czechoslovakia, 1870s. Private collection.

33   Knitted woolen purse. La Paz, Bolivia, before 1910.

34   Dolls, maize ears and fabric. Fulbe tribe, Saré Doundou village, Senegal, 1969.

35   Rag doll, bast skirt, eyes of kauri, hair of horsehair; schoolchildren's work. Lomé, Togo, before 1983.

36   Slingshots,
(A) wool. Mapuche tribe, Coipuco village, Cautín province, Chile, before 1972.
(B) sisal. Fulbe, Saré Doundou village, Senegal, 1969.

37   Boomerangs, wood. Queensland, Australia, 19th century (according to McCarthy, 1962, 17, 24).

38   Hoop, twig and string. U.S. Southwest, 1930-31.

39   'Cat's cradle' figures of thread or string:
(A) Fish trap. Patomana tribe, Guyana, early 20th century (according to Lutz, 1912, 11).
(B) Trouser legs. Scotland, early 20th century (according to Gray, 1903, 117-118).
(C, D) Young girl and monkey's tail. Injour region, eastern Nigeria, early 20th century (according to Dayrell, 1912, 136-138).

40   Ship model, reed and wood. Aymaras,

Suriki Islands in Lake Titicaca, Bolivia, before 1964.

41 (A) Catamaran, wood. Apamama, Gilbert Islands, Micronesia, end of 19th century (according to Krämer, 1906, 290-291).
(B) Catamaran, wood. Truk Islands, Micronesia, end of 19th century (according to Krämer, 1932, 241-242).
(C) Raft, wood. Tetua, Nonouti, Gilbert Islands, Micronesia, end of 19th century (according to Koch, 1965, 170, Abb. 105).

42 Doll with a leather head, body and clothes of fabric, wearing glass beads. Dakotas, U.S.A., before 1929.

43 Leopard and antelope, dried meat, covered with animal skin. Hausa, Nigeria, 1970s.

44 Scooter, stained wood. Ibana village in Ruwenzori Mountains, Uganda, before 1980.

45 (A) So-called hen, dried clay with leather strap. Qara Chodzha, eastern Turkestan, China, early 20th century. Museum für Völkerkunde, Berlin (according to Coq, 1916, 14, Fig. 7).
(B) Balance, wood with polychrome decoration and metal. Quebec, Canada, 1860-70. A. A. Rockefeller Folk Art Coll., Williamsburg, Virginia, U.S.A. (according to Lipman-Winchester, 1974, 181, Fig. 231).

46 'Cabinet-maker's hedgehog', wood. Valašsko (Walachia), Moravia, 1970s. Private collection.

47 Figures of children, painted wood. Erzgebirge, Bohemia, before 1945. Private collection.

48 Movable dolls (so-called *Hampelmann*), polychrome wood:
(A) Soldier. Germanisches Nationalmuseum, Munich, 19th century (according to Gröber-Metzger, 1965, Abb. 54).
(B) Tirolean figure. Bought in Königsee in 1984, modern replica of a folk toy from the Berchtesgaden area. Private collection.

49 Horse on wheels, wood with polychrome decoration, reconstruction. Odenwald, Germany, 1980. Private collection.

50 Doll, polychrome wood. Val di Gardena, Italy, 19th century. Musée de l'Homme, Paris (according to Anonymous 1964, 115).

51 Baby doll, wood with remnants of polychrome decoration. Bohemia, second half of 19th century. Private collection.

52 Infant, wood. Usedom locality, Germany, 11th century. Deutches Spielzeugmuseum, Sonneberg (according to Bachmann-Hausmann, 1971, Fig. 13).

53 Horse rider with pendulum, wood, partial polychrome decoration. Seiffen, Germany, 1960. Ethnographic Museum, Prague.

54 Three-masted ship on wheels, wood and paper. Erzgebirge, Bohemia, before 1899. Ethnographic Museum, Prague.

55 Candleholder and nutcracker, polychrome wood. Seiffen, Germany, c. 1900. Spielzeugmuseum, Seiffen (according to Bilz, 1983, 68).

56 Miniature kitchen, wood with polychrome decoration. Seiffen, Germany, current production, 1984. Private collection.

57 Pigeon-house, wood and paper with polychrome decoration. Seiffen region, Germany, c. 1898 (according to Just-Karpinski, 1982, Abb. 121).

58 Riding school, wood and paper with polychrome decoration. Seiffen region, Germany, 1918 (according to Just-Karpinski, 1982, Abb. 122).

59 Rocking horses, wood with polychrome decoration. Eisfeld locality, Thuringia. Germany, c. 1820, 1860 and 1900 (according to Schmolitzky, 1964, Abb. 78-80).

60 Rider on a rocking horse, wood with polychrome decoration. Seiffen, Germany, 19th to 20th century. Staatliches Museum für Volkskunst, Dresden (according to Fritzsch-Bachmann, 1977, tab. 34).

61 Baby dolls, wood with polychrome decoration. Skašov, Bohemia, before 1945. Ethnographic Museum, Prague.

62 Whistle with pinwheel, wood with polychrome decoration. Klatovy district, Bohemia, before 1945. Museum of Decorative Arts, Prague.

63 Miniature rocking horses, wood with polychrome decoration. Uherské Hradiště, Moravia, before 1940. Museum of Decorative Arts, Prague.

64 Jar decorated with motif of a children's festive procession showing a kite, porcelain. Qing Dynasty, China, 1644-1912.

65 Miniature village and animals wood with polychrome decoration. Erzgebirge, Bo-

hemia, before 1978. Ethnographic Museum, Prague.

66   Figure of an officer, wood with polychrome decoration. Tirolean-Bavarian area, first half of 19th century. Museum of Decorative Arts, Prague.

67   Rooster or peacock on wheels, wood with polychrome decoration. Val di Gardena, Italy, before 1941. Ethnographic Museum, Prague.

68   Clapper-doll, wood with polychrome decoration. Erzgebirge, Bohemia, before 1939. Museum of Decorative Arts, Prague.

69   Miniature rack wagon and mail coach, both with teams of horses, wood with polychrome decoration. Seiffen, Germany, before 1961. Private collection.

70   Genre figures, wood with polychrome decoration. Skašov, Bohemia, before 1945. Ethnographic Museum, Prague.

71   Military bugler on a horse, wood with polychrome decoration. Skašov, Bohemia, first quarter of 20th century. Ethnographic Museum, Prague.

72   Pull-along cart, wood with polychrome decoration. Poland, before 1961. Ethnographic Museum, Prague.

73   Bird whistle, wood with polychrome decoration. Slovakia, before 1926. Museum of Decorative Arts, Prague.

74   Walking figures, polychrome wood. Chlum near Hartmanice, Bohemia, 1920s. Private collection.

75   Pull-along cart, painted wood. Acquired in 1941 in Russia, probably made in the Ukraine or Poland. Ethnographic Museum, Prague.

76   Nest of dolls, wood with polychrome decoration. Russia, c. 1890. Museum of Childhood, Edinburgh (according to Fraser, 1966, 156, Fig. 182).

77   Samovar, wood with painting. Yaroslavl district, Russia, before 1901. Ethnographic Museum, Prague.

78   Horses, wood with polychrome decoration. Dalarna district, Sweden, before 1938. Museum of Decorative Arts, Prague.

79   Cradle, wood. Sarajevo, Bosnia and Herzegovina, c. 1901. Ethnographic Museum, Prague.

80   Doll, wood with polychrome decoration. Italy, 17th century. Musée des Arts Décoratifs, Paris (according to Fraser, 1966, Fig. 82).

81   Doll, wood. Narainpur village, Medinipur district, Bengal, India, 1976.

82   Tiger, wood with polychrome decoration. Puri, Orissa state, India, before 1976.

83   Jacob's ladder, coloured wood and fabric. Catalonia, Spain, 1970s. Private collection.

84   (A) Bilboquet, wood with polychrome decoration. Savantvadi district, India, 1870s. (B) Bilboquet, wood with polychrome decoration, Mexico, before 1982.

85   Rattle and clapper-drum, wood and leather with polychrome decoration and lacquer. The rattle of unknown origin, the drum from Orissa, India, before 1878.

86   Hand-mill and rattle, wood with lacquered polychrome decoration. Savantvadi district, India, 1878.

87   Doll, wood with polychrome decoration. Japan, before 1961.

88   Tiger and yearling, lacquered wood. Japan, before 1925.

89   Puppet, painted wood. Bijogo, Bissagos Islands, 1920s.

90   Rooster and quail, painted wood. Japan, before 1925.

91   Figures of the emperor and empress, wood with polychrome decoration. Japan, before 1945.

92   Dolls, stained wood. Mossi tribe, Upper Volta, 20th century. Segy Gallery, New York (according to Segy, 1975, 326, Fig. 461).

93   Soldiers on a pantograph, wood with polychrome decoration. Russia, before 1896. Ethnographic Museum, Prague.

94   Smiths — mechanical toy, wood with polychrome decoration. Russia, before 1896. Ethnographic Museum, Prague.

95   Rooster, wood with polychrome decoration. Sweden, before 1938. Museum of Decorative Arts, Prague.

96   Dolls, wood and pulp with polychrome decoration. Western Bengal, India. The taller doll comes from the Vishnupur district, before 1962.

97 Figure of a milkseller, wood and papier mâché with polychrome decoration. Madras, India, before 1955.

98 Figures of a camel and elephant, wood with polychrome decoration. Jaipur, Rajasthan, India, before 1878.

99 Ink pot in the shape of a peacock, wood with polychrome decoration. Udaipur, India, before 1958.

100 Cart with team of oxen, painted plywood. Rangoon, Burma, before 1969.

101 Doll, wood with polychrome decoration, painting in clay. Kanuri, Nigeria, 1974. Private collection.

102 Stylized doll, painted wood. Yoruba, Nigeria, before 1968.

103 Doll, wood with polychrome decoration. Ibo or Ibibio, Nigeria, before 1967.

104 Doll, stained wood. Signed 'Hamba of Shamusengo'. Kuba, Kahembe region, Zaire, before 1949.

105 Dolls, raffia palm pulp and hammered bark. Ubangi-Shari River basin, Zaire, before 1949.

106 Dolls, wood, partly stained. South African Republic.
(A) Chopi tribe,
(B) Gwamba tribe,
(C) Venda tribe.
Transvaal Museum (according to Anonymous, *Illustrated*, 1935, 1188, Fig. 1-2).

107 Elephant, wood with burned pattern and staining. Luba, Zaire, before 1966.

108 'Russian' (big) wheel, painted plywood. Oaxaca or Ciudad de Mexico areas, Mexico, before 1982.

109 *Kachina*, wood with polychrome decoration. The upper figure probably represents the spirit of Kau. Hopi, New Mexico, U.S.A., before 1893.

110 Papoose for a doll, wood with relief carving, fabric, embroidered with porcupine quills. Dakotas, U.S.A., before 1856.

111 Lorry, wood with polychrome decoration. Mexico, before 1982.

112 Easter rattles, wood with polychrome decoration and lacquer. Xochimilco, Mexico, before 1982.

113 Miniature guitar, wood with polychrome decoration. Mexico, before 1982.

114 Ox-drawn wagons, all of wood with polychrome decoration.
(A) Nuremberg, 19th century (according to Hercík, 1951, 55, Pl. CXXVI).
(B) Berchtesgaden, modern copy of a traditional toy. Museum of Childhood, Edinburgh (according to Fraser, 1966, Fig. 15).
(C) Northeastern Poland, 20th century. Museum of Decorative Arts, Prague (according to Hercík, 1951, 54, Pl. CXIX).
(D) Yavorovo village, Lvov district, Ukraine, 1950s. Author V. Priyma. Ethnographic Museum, Kiev (according to Collective, 1976, Fig. 31).
The second wagon from the same village. Kustarny muzei, Moscow (according to Hercík, 1951, 54, Pl. CXII).

115 Pull-along horses,
(A) wood with polychrome decoration. Vologda area, Russia, 20th century. Gosudarstvenny istorichesky muzei, Moscow (according to Anonymous, 1979 a, Fig. 160).
(B) wood. Egypt, Roman period. British Museum, London (according to Hercík, 1951, 27).
(C) wood with polychrome decoration. Near Domažlice, Bohemia, 20th century. Domažlice Museum.

116 Tiger with two Chinese, wood with polychrome decoration. China, before 1957.

117 (A) Monkey on a ladder, wood with polychrome decoration. China, before 1956.
(B) Gymnast on a trapeze, wood with polychrome decoration. Mexico, before 1982.
(C) Tiger, lacquer on a wooden core. Mexico, before 1982.
(D) Tiger and monkey, ceramic with wood and polychrome decoration. China, 19th century.
(E) Gymnast on strings, wood with polychrome decoration. Mexico, before 1982.

118 Rattle in the shape of a tiger's head, wood with polychrome decoration. China, before 1965.

119 Drummer-clapper, wood with polychrome decoration. China, before 1956.

120 Tiger with two Chinese — mechanical toy, wood with polychrome decoration. China, before 1957.

121 Nest of Darumas, wood with polychrome decoration. Japan, before 1906.

122 Horse — votive gift, wooden board with polychrome decoration. From the Muramatsu

sanctuary in Tokai village, Ibaraki prefecture, Japan, before 1969.

123   Clapper in the shape of a lion's head, wood with polychrome decoration. Japan, before 1925.

124   Quail on wheels, wood with polychrome decoration. Setaka in Fukuoka prefecture, Kyü-shü Island, Japan, before 1969.

125   Small chest with lid, wood with polychrome decoration. Hitoyoshi in Kumamoto prefecture, Kyü-shü Island, Japan, before 1969.

126   Parrot, wood with polychrome decoration. Bohemia, before 1945. Ethnographic Museum, Prague.

127   Pots, glazed ceramic. Koloveč, Bohemia, before 1913.

128   Dishes and animals, smoked and polished ceramic. Quinchamalí, Chile, before 1938.

129   Doll with infant, ceramic and fabric. Guatemala, 1970s. Private collection.

130   Small items, glazed ceramic. The basket is from Galicia, Ukraine, the jug from Russia, end of 19th century. Ethnographic Museum, Prague.

131   Set of birds, unglazed ceramic. Tunja village, Colombia, 1930s.

132   Doll, ceramic. Nuremberg, Germany 15th century, Deutsches Spielzeugmuseum, Sonneberg (according to Bachmann-Hausmann, 1971, Fig. 50).

133   Knight on a horse, ceramic. Striegau locality, Silesia, second half of 14th century (according to Burian, 1962, 307).

134   Boat on wheels, fired clay. Warka locality, Iraq, 7th century B.C. Deutches Arch. Inst. Baghdad (according to Náprstek Museum Photo Archives).

135   Whistles — birds, polished and fired ceramic. Central Mexico, before 1900.

136   Domestic fowl, ceramic with painting on a plaster base. Dymkovo village (today Kirov), Russia, before 1945. Author: J. Z. Koshkina. Ethnographic Museum, Prague.

137   Figural whistles, ceramic, slip-painting or glaze.
(A)   Skorping locality, Jutland, Denmark, early 20th century.

(B)   Lorca locality, Murica, Spain, 1972.
(C)   Colmar, Alsace, France, 1906.
(D)   Agram locality, Croatia, early 20th century.
(E)   Barcelos locality, Portugal, mid-20th century.
(F)   Dymkovo (today Kirov), Russia 1971.
(G)   Rumania, before 1972. Private collection.
(H)   Stara Sil village, Sambir district, Ukraine, early 20th century.
[All, with the exception of (G), according to Nixdorf, 1974.]

138   Vase seller, glazed ceramic. Spain, before 1894. Ethnographic Museum, Prague.

139   Horseback rider, ceramic with slip painting. China, before 1965.

140   Human figures and a horse, painted and lacquered ceramic. Egra village, Bengal, India, 1976.

141   Snake, bamboo sections with polychrome decoration. Japan, before 1925.

142   Animals, wood with polychrome decoration. Ibo or Ibibio, Nigeria, before 1968.

143   Doll with movable arms, wood with polychrome decoration. Ibibio, Nigeria, before 1968.

144   Doll on circular base, glazed ceramic. Stupava, Slovakia, before 1945. Ethnographic Museum, Prague.

145   Dishes, glazed ceramic. Quezaltenango, Guatemala, before 1914.

146   Money-boxes, glazed ceramic. Quezaltenango, Guatemala, before 1914.

147   Doll, glazed ceramic. Cochabamba, Bolivia, before 1964.

148   Genre figures, glazed ceramic. Domažlice, Bohemia, before 1945. Ethnographic Museum, Prague.

149   Figure of a tortoise, ceramic, painted with white clay. Shipibo, Venezuela, before 1985. Private collection.

150   Figures of bears, ceramic. Santa Clara Pueblo, New Mexico, U.S.A., 1930-31.

151   Rattles in the form of a bird and kitten, ceramic. China, before 1956.

152   Musicians, painted ceramic, fabric whiskers. China, before 1965.

153 Lion, painted ceramic. China, before 1965.

154 Whistles in the form of a rider and animals, painted and glazed ceramic. Dog and rider — Ukraine, before 1914; ram — Russia, before 1889. Ethnographic Museum, Prague.

155 Model of a hut, ceramic with slip-painting. Uvongo village, Zulu, South Africa, 1970s.

156 Rider and horses, glazed and unglazed ceramic. Cochabamba, Bolivia, 1964.

157 Animals on wheels, ceramic. Huamantla locality, Tlaxcala, Mexico, A.D. 800—1250. Museum of the American Indian, New York, U.S.A. (according to Dockstader, 1965, Fig. 47).

158 Bread of the dead. Mexico, before 1982.

159 (A) Sturgeon (?), gingerbread. Gorodtse village, Russia, 19th century (according to Náprstek Museum Photo Archives).
(B) Dough figures. Pacov, Bohemia, 19th century. Klatovy Museum (according to Hercík, 1951, 42, Pl. XXVI).
(C) Bread figures. Wallis canton, Switzerland, 19th century. Schweizerisches Museum für Volkskunde, Basle (according to Bachmann, 1971, Fig. 70).

160 Horse, cheese. Poland, mid-20th century (according to Traser, 1966, Fig. 16).

161 Baby doll, painted papier mâché. Zagorsk, Russia, before 1945. Ethnographic Museum, Prague.

162 Castle, cardboard and printed paper. Erzgebirge, Bohemia, 1880-90. Private collection.

163 Driver, buggy and horse, painted paper, wood. Zagorsk, Russia, before 1945. Ethnographic Museum, Prague.

164 Dolls, painted papier mâché. Coyoacán, Mexico, before 1982.

165 Figures of tiger and monkey, painted and lacquered ceramic. China, before 1965.

166 Child with a pomegranate, painted ceramic. China, before 1965.

167 Models of buildings, porcelain with enamel. Qing-dao, China, 1950s.

168 Figures, sugar. Michoacán, Mexico, before 1982.

169 Jigsaw puzzle, printed paper. Germany, end of 19th century. Private collection.

170 Miniature monk's hat, papier mâché. Rangoon, Burma, before 1969.

171 Elephant carrying a Chinese child, painted papier mâché. Kyü-shü Island, Japan, 1970s. Private collection.

172 Market place, cardboard and printed paper. Bohemia, end of 19th century. Private collection.

173 Raspberry blowers, printed paper. Bohemia, 1970s. Private collection.

174 Grim Reaper, painted papier mâché. Celaya, Mexico, before 1982.

175 Page from a 'Circus' accordion book, coloured print on paper. Bohemia, second half of 19th century. Private collection.

176 Masks, painted palm leaves. Central Sumatra, Indonesia, early 20th century (according to Maas, 1909, 162).

177 Married farm couple, coloured straw. Sweden, 1930s. Museum of Decorative Arts, Prague.

178 Basket with lid, painted and lacquered straw. China, before 1965.

179 Tortoise on wheels, palm leaves with painting. Java, Indonesia, before 1945.

180 Basket, straw. China, before 1965.

181 Animals, plaited palm fibres. China, before 1965.

182 Miniature basket for winnowing rice, coloured straw. Bengal, before 1960.

183 (A) Doll, dried maize husks. Thailand, 20th century. Museum für Völkerkunde, Leipzig (according to Bachmann-Hausmann, 1971, Fig. 28).
(B) Doll, maize ear and dried maize husks. Mexico, 20th century. Musée d'Ethnographie, Neuchâtel (according to Bachmann-Hausmann, 1971, Fig. 22).

184 Baskets, split osiers. Bolivia, before 1937.

185 Animals, coloured raffia palm fibres. Ibibio, Nigeria, before 1968.

186 Doll, grass. Tanzania, second half of 19th century. Museum für Völkerkunde, Berlin (according to Ratzel, 1888, 112).

187 Basket, plaited and painted split osiers, souvenir inscription. Helsingborg, Sweden, 1905. Museum of Decorative Arts, Prague.

188 Rattle, plaited and painted split osiers. Crimean Tatars, Simferopol, Ukraine, before 1899.

189 Figure, moss and pine cones. Russia, 19th century. Deutsches Spielzeugmuseum, Sonneberg (according to Bachmann-Hausmann, 1971, Fig. 233).

190 Doll, birch bark. Sweden, 19th century. Deutsches Spielzeugmuseum, Sonneberg (according to Bachmann-Hausmann, 1971, Fig. 68).

191 Doll, calabash decorated with engraving. Zaramo tribe, Tanzania, 1944-47. Dar es-Salaam Museum (according to Harding, 1961, 73, Fig. 4).

192 Dolls, reindeer pelt. Chukchi, Siberia, Russia, early 20th century. Etnografichesky muzei narodov SSSR (according to Kaplan, 1974, Fig. 54).

193 Soldiers, painted tin. Germany, end of 19th century. Museum of Decorative Arts, Prague.

194 Tin figure. France, 13th century. Musée de Cluny, Paris (according to Fraser, 1966, 60, Fig. 68).

195 Kaleidoscope, printed paper and coloured glass. China, before 1956.

196 Horse, painted papier mâché. Mexico City, Mexico, before 1982.

197 Skull, painted papier mâché. Mexico City, Mexico, before 1982.

198 Grim Reaper, painted papier mâché. Mexico City, Mexico, before 1982.

199 Indian, plaited plant roots. Arizona or New Mexico area, U.S.A., 1920s.

200 Mounted rider with beast of burden, coloured straw, maize husks and wood. Santa Maria de Chigmecatitlán, Mexico, before 1982.

201 Figures from an 'English Hunt' set, painted tin. Nuremberg, Germany, 19th century. Museum of Decorative Arts, Prague.

202 Carp, coloured fabric. China, before 1956.

203 Chinese lantern in the shape of a lion,

silk on wired frame. China, before 1965.

204 Figure of a llama, limestone. La Paz, Bolivia, 1910.

205 (A) Dolls made of string. Beni Hasan, Egypt, period of Middle Kingdom, c. 2000 B.C. (according to Garstang, 1903, 130, Pl. I). (B) Dolls, wood and cotton. Chankai Culture, Peru, 13th-15th century. The first doll — Náprstek Museum, Prague, the second — private collection (according to Náprstek Museum Photo Archives).

206 Figure of a magician, fabric, painted face. Made by Hausa women in Tripoli, Libya, 1880.

207 Miniature containers, brass. India, before 1878.

208 Rag dolls. Bihar, India, 20th century. The first pair from the Crafts Museum of New Delhi (according to Mookerjee, 1968, Pl. XXII); the second — Sheikpura, Gaya locality. Acuntosh Museum (according to Pal, 1962, 26).

209 Cyclist on a two-wheeler, wire and cloth. Harare, Mashons, Zimbabwe, acquired 1989.

210 Doll, glass beads and fabric. Zulu, South Africa, early 1980s.

211 Doll, cloth and palm substance. Seminole, Florida, U.S.A., 1960s. Private collection.

212 Horse and ibex, wool and wood. Addis Ababa, Ethiopia, acquired 1988.

213 Miniature leather sandals. Bought in La Paz, Bolivia, before 1937.

214 Dolls representing married couple, impregnated and painted fabric stiffened with paper. Gwalior, Madha Pradesh state, India, 1980.

215 Doll, fabric, glass buttons, painted face. Navaho, U.S.A., 1930-31.

216 'One-actor theatre':
(A) Play about Hercules, miniature from the book by Johan de Grice 'Romance of Alexander', 13th-14th century. Bodleian Library, Oxford (according to Fraser, 1966, 66, Fig. 76).
(B) Glove puppet theatre. Bohemia, 19th century (according to Zíbrt, 1906, 96).
(C) Touring theatre, woodcut. Japan, 19th century (according to Hilská, 1947, Fig. XXXIX).

217 Marionettes from a 'family' puppet theatre. A. Münzberg Co., Prague, Bohemia, 1930s-1950s. Private collection.

218 Shadow puppets and props, painted leather:
(A) Boat with archers. Egypt, 19th century. Private collection.
(B) Chest. Sarajevo, Yugoslavia, 19th century. Private collection.
(C) Night watchman. Turkey, 19th century. Theater-Museum, Kiel.
(D) Soldier Arnaut Tuzsuz Deli Bekir. Turkey, 19th century. Private collection.
(E) Rider. Alepo, Syria. Islamisches Museum, Berlin.
(F) Karagöz. Istanbul, Turkey, 19th century.
[(A−E) according to Jacob, 1925, 105, 113 at 122, at 130, at 144.]

219 Shadow puppet, goatskin painted with organic colours. Andhra Pradesh, India, end of 19th-early 20th century.

220 Marionette, wood with polychrome decoration and fabric. Udaipur, Rajasthan, India, 1970s. Private collection.

221 Marionettes, wood with polychrome decoration and fabric. Mandalay, Burma, before 1969.

223 Miniature rod puppets, painted modelling material. China, before 1956.

224 Glove puppets, coloured fabric. Mexico, before 1961.

225 Rod puppet, painted plywood. Oaxaca region or Mexico City, Mexico, before 1982.

226 Costume doll, wood with polychrome decoration and fabric. Japan, 1970s. Private collection.

227 Costume dolls, coloured fabric. Bolivia, before 1964.

228 Shadow puppets, painted leather. China, 20th century.

229 Puppet, stained wood. Bambara, Mali, 1970s.

230 Jack-in-the-box. U.S.A., 19th century. New York Historical Museum (according to Fraser, 1966, 167).

231 Doll, wood, fabric, wax, costume jewellery. Sudan, before 1911.

232 Baby doll in a papoose and an American Indian, fabric and plaster. U.S.A., end of 19th century.

233 Dolls, coloured leather. Afrikaner, South Africa, before 1880.

234 American Indian, wood, decorated with burned pattern and feathers. Xingu River basin, Brazil, 1970s.

235 Model of two-storeyed building with hay loft. Alpine region, Austria, c. 1930.

236 Village house, wood with polychrome decoration. Jedlina village, Bohemia, 1925. Private collection.

237 Furniture, wood with polychrome decoration. Bohemia, 1920s. Private collection.

238 Building set, wood. Zagreb, Yugoslavia, 1966. Author: F. Uršič (according to Anonymous, 1969, Fig. 123)

Index

239